THE
CRAFT
OF
INVESTING

THE
CRAFT
OF
INVESTING

JOHN TRAIN

HarperBusiness
A Division of HarperCollinsPublishers

A hardcover edition of this book was published in 1994 by Harper Business, a division of HarperCollins Publishers.

First paperback edition published 1995.

Designed by Alma Hochhauser Orenstein

The Library of Congress has catalogued the hardcover edition as follows:

Train, John.
    The craft of investing / by John Train. — 1st ed.
      p. cm.
    Includes index.
    ISBN 0-88730-626-8
    1. Stocks. 2. Investments. I. Title.
  HG4661.T72   1994
  332.6—dc20   94-6856

ISBN 0-88730-761-2 (pbk.)
95 96 97 98 99 AC/RRD 10 9 8 7 6 5 4 3 2 1

Contents

Acknowledgments

My thanks to Sara Perkins, for editorial advice; and Kenneth Lubbock, Peter Scott, Virginia Armat Hurt, Henry Babcock, Alexandra Ourousoff, Winthrop Knowlton, Celia Hensman, Nina Train Choa, and Lisa Train for their comments.

I have adapted some material from columns in *Forbes*, *Harvard Magazine*, and the *New York Times*, to all of which I am grateful.

Foreword

When I was a boy I spent some time on a ranch in Montana. On Saturday nights we would drive into town to a cozy tavern where there was a perpetual poker game. This arrangement provided the house with two advantages from which it profited mightily. First, it sold whiskey to the players, and second, it furnished a permanent dealer—a girl, as it happened—who didn't drink herself. The cowboys' mission was to have a good time after a tough week. Hers was to make money for her employer. She knew the odds, and almost always pulled further and further ahead as the night wore on and the cowboys, lubricated by booze, became ever jollier and more prone to exciting but illogical bets.

In all games the difference between the amateur and the professional is that the professional plays the odds, while the amateur, whether he realizes it or not, is among other things a thrill seeker. Investment, too, is part a science and part a game, and just as in poker, you need to sort out your motives. The essence of the whole matter is buying a company in the market for less than its appraised value. Fortunately, most of the other investment players are quite emotional, so if you are thorough and patient, you can find good deals. However, they will rarely be easy, since many other people are looking for the same thing. Thus, to prosper in the investment game, as in any other, requires that you be *right*—so you'll win—and *different*—so you'll get attractive odds. I hope that this book will help you do that.*

---

* You can also learn a lot from Andrew Tobias's *The Only Investment Guide You'll Ever Need* (and its successors) and Benjamin Graham's *The Intelligent Investor*, partic-

In the opening section I will briefly discuss several major investment styles, to give an idea of what they involve. The reader can then select one or more that conform to his or her temperament and the information available. Just as when investing in a foreign country, one should look for its area of natural advantage—U.S. agriculture and Japanese consumer electronics, for instance, rather than vice versa—so too the investor should look inward at his background, temperament, and circumstances to see what comes naturally to him.

I do not discuss modern portfolio theory, the use of derivatives, and mathematical models because I observe that the great investors don't use them, the private investor doesn't need them, and they do not in fact improve performance. They seem instead to flatten performance at some cost.

The challenge of building family capital involves handling real estate, works of art, and other specialized assets. Also coping with taxes and trust law, and getting the younger generation of a family involved in its affairs. So these subjects are covered, too. Finally, since most things go wrong (see number 4 of "Train's Laws"), I have included some admonitions and cautionary tales.

---

ularly the "conclusion" at the very end. *One Up on Wall Street: How to Use What You Already Know to Make Money in the Market,* by Peter Lynch and John Rothchild, is extremely informative, although it makes profiting from consumer trends seem less challenging than some may find it in practice. The old Gerald M. Loeb classic, *The Battle for Investment Survival,* is dated, and pushes the stockbroker's favorite tactic of medium-term trading. Burton Malkiel's popular *A Random Walk Down Wall Street* espouses the (false) efficient market theory, which I note with satisfaction he has refuted by going into the business himself, and beating the averages. Fred Schwed's *Where Are the Customers' Yachts?* (illustrated by Peter Arno!) is a delight.

Bad books on investing make it sound easy.

PART 1

The Craft

The Craft of the Specific

Everyone needs to preserve savings for future use; that is, to invest. There are two ways: by owning assets with reasonably predictable earnings, such as company shares or real estate; or else by lending the money, such as by depositing it in a bank or buying a bond. Stocks offer a much higher return over long periods than bank deposits or bonds, and smaller companies a higher return than very large companies. (*Speculating* is buying something with an unpredictable return but which you hope will "go up.") In this book I talk principally about owning assets represented by marketable securities: that is, investing in stocks.

There are two basic techniques that I believe most investors can follow with a good hope of success, and which are the subjects of later chapters.

RETURNS[1] ON ALTERNATIVE INVESTMENTS: 1926–1993

	Total Return %	Real Return %
Stocks	10.3	7.0
Small stocks	12.4	8.9
Corporate bonds	5.6	2.4
Government bonds	5.0	1.8
Treasury bills	3.7	0.5
Inflation	3.1	0

[1] Compound average return.
Source: Ibbotson Associates

First, buy growth stocks during market washouts and hold them until their growth slows.

Alternatively, buy conventional companies when they are selling extremely cheaply in the market, and sell them again when they have recovered.

To follow either of these techniques requires common sense and a feeling for the world, together with a certain amount of analytical ability. (There are also always new techniques, some of which I will touch on later, but which are *much* harder to execute.) While an investment professional must know a great many things, it is sufficient for the private investor to know just a few. One good buy a year, or even every few years, is enough so that you will prosper mightily.

Your investment odds improve, and your risk declines correspondingly, to the extent that you know more than the market does about a stock you are buying. You can do that either through superior knowledge of something specific, like a shopper who spots a bargain, or by recognizing that a whole class of stocks, such as Mexican companies in the 1980s (which have since risen dozens of times in dollar terms), is too far out of favor and buying a package of them. The general rule is this: *Investment opportunity is the difference between the reality and the perception.* Thus, *all good investors are contrarians.* Any publicly traded market will swing wildly back and forth between euphoria and despair. So if you can get the facts right, buying good value that is out of vogue will do very well for you.

Investment, as distinct from speculation, is *the craft of the specific.* It's extraordinary how much time the public spends on the unknowable. Is the market going up or down? Is the economy recovering? What is the government going to do? In military matters, it is notorious that armchair tacticians talk about grand strategy, while professionals talk about supply. The most elegant strategy will fail if the army runs out of food, fuel, or ammunition. Similarly, large conceptions are cheap in the investment business. *What you really need to know is whether company A is superior to company B, and whether their prices reflect that difference.*

When one does *not* know the values, one starts guessing vaguely how a stock is likely to move in the short term, which is unknowable and not even useful. The long term is important and also easy: *as a company's earnings and intrinsic value rise over the years, its stock will infallibly follow.* Admittedly, short-term movements are interesting. You see tables showing that if you could have caught interim highs and lows you would have done much better than the averages. Sure! But that sort of movement—Brownian motion, practically—is virtually unpredictable, and expensive to try to take advantage of because of high transactional costs.

And consider this: The total return from owning U.S. stocks for very long periods has been about 9½ to 10 percent, market crashes included. However the greatest moments are usually the violent rebounds from a bottom. But market timers are usually out of stocks at a bottom, and *if you miss the best month or so in each decade, you cut your return by about half!*

Furthermore, if, like a tape watcher in the old days, you spend your time worrying about short-term market jiggles, you will deflect your attention from what can make you rich: how well your companies are doing.

To sum up, you should forget the short term, and not worry about the economy or the direction of the market. Instead, *buy a share of a company the way you buy a house: because you know all about it, and want to own it for a long time at that price.* In fact, you should only buy what you would be happy to own *in the absence of any market.*

Focus

In managing your investments, the principle of conservation of energy becomes central, *since to win you have to know more than the market does about some particular company you are buying stock in.* If, on the contrary, you try to know about practically everything, you will probably know less than the market about any particular company. So one of the decisions you need to make is what to focus on. Most investors give this subject little thought. And yet the decision to concentrate on growth, value, emerging markets, exotica, distressed securities, high technology, small or regional companies, real estate, high-grade bonds, low-grade bonds, or whatever is central to your success. Think of yourself as a company: A company almost never succeeds in manufacturing a variety of unrelated products, all the way from building materials to chewing gum. Rather, it eventually identifies an area of strength, and seeks to succeed in that market and build out from there. The same with venture capital. Early in their careers, aspiring venture capitalists may be prepared to sit in an office considering any deal that comes across the desk. Then, either they lose their money, or they eventually specialize to the point where they have learned enough about some particular area to be able to distinguish the rare valid proposition from the hundreds that don't qualify.

As I will describe, it is often possible to determine which categories of investment are attractively priced at any time—growth, value, high technology, one or another foreign market, and so forth; that factor should also be given considerable weight, since the mispricing usually remains in effect for a number of years. *Thus, the investor must be both realistic and flexible, since change is the one thing he can depend on.* Companies change, the economy changes, society changes, countries change, and the composition of the market changes.

There are two ways to analyze stocks. First, you appraise the whole company as one unit the way you appraise a house: What have similar properties sold for recently? What's the replacement cost? What's the original cost minus depreciation? And for a commercial property, what's the earning power? Just as there are appraisers of houses, there are investment bankers who appraise, and indeed deal in, whole companies, as well as executives in corporate acquisition departments who evaluate other companies in their industry. And, for some industries, services that calculate company takeover values. Such specialists often know quite accurately what an enterprise is worth in the market. So if, for instance, an oil company has 20 million shares selling at $20 a share, implying a market capitalization of $400 million, and if your specialist tells you that an informed buyer would probably pay $800 million for it, or $40 a share, then you've found a good bet. This is the way a wheeler-dealer buys a company: What's the whole shebang worth as it stands?

The second analytical technique is needed when such large-scale expert knowledge is not available; it is called security analysis, taught in textbooks and business schools. It works well too. In this book I describe some simplified but effective ways of doing that analytical job. It will not turn the reader into a certified financial analyst able to take apart any company's figures. There are courses for that. But he should become able to find a few very good stocks with reasonable confidence in his method, or alternatively he will learn how to evaluate what his professional advisor is doing for him.

Investment is a game, and calls for the same qualities required to win at any game: You have to love the game and have an intense desire to win. Whatever strategy you follow, you should follow three rules: Be thorough, tough-minded, and flexible; know a great deal about any company you buy into; and only buy when the company is misunderstood by the market.

As to the first rule, you either have that cast of mind or not. If not, don't attempt to do it yourself. Hire a pro. As to the second, you can easily do quite a lot of the work yourself *if you have a basic knowledge of accounting*, the language of business, and of the structure of American industry. Otherwise you are just pecking at popular notions, a losing strategy. This book should help make the third rule, buying when a company is misunderstood, easier for you.

Growth Investing: A Field of Acorns

In the next chapters I will describe several investment approaches, since somewhat different techniques are appropriate for each. The first—and for most investors the basic one, the way the red Bordeaux are the foundation of a wine cellar—is owning shares in growing enterprises. This might be compared to buying a field planted with seedlings and watching them grow into mature trees. *If you stay with a collection of strongly growing enterprises year after year, you will in time become rich.* When I meet someone who has prospered as an investor, I usually find that he bought an interest in a few growing companies and held on for ten or fifteen years. He got to know them intimately, and watched some of them rise tenfold. That's how my own clients have invariably done it. One gets on the up escalator of earnings and dividends and stays there. One penalty of growth investing is low initial yield. But surprisingly enough, a growth stock, whose dividends rise rapidly will eventually give you a much higher yield than an "income" stock whose dividends aren't growing as fast. The other penalty is volatility. As I observe many times in this book, you just have to accept it. Look at ADP: Many times, the stock dropped over 20 percent. You just had to ride through the dips, relying on the earnings to bail you out.

Most good companies have phases, like people: infancy, youth, maturity, and senescence. So do entire industries: railroads, steel companies, utilities, automobiles, and mainframe computers were all hot growth sectors that became low-margin competitive arenas when their business franchises eroded. *Central to growth investing is participation in the growth phase of a company, or in the growth phase of an industry, or in both together.*

A remarkably good index of a growth company is its *return on reinvested capital.* Often it can put its cash flow back to work at a return of 15 or 20 percent, or more. That's a much better deal for the investor than paying the money out in a taxable dividend. In fact, *the privilege of staying aboard a growth stock for a long time as it compounds its earnings at a high rate is one of the great attractions of portfolio investing.*

But can one actually pick growth stocks in practice? Yes, sometimes (see the appendix "Great Growth Stocks"). Growth stocks are typically found in one of two ways: First, *identify an industry with a brilliant future and buy stock in a few of its strongest companies.* Or second, quite differently, *spot specialized growth companies wherever they happen to be, even in dull industries.* Here are some aspects of each technique.

Leaders in growth industries: During recent decades you did not have to be a genius to spot the potential of computers, semiconductors, oil-field service companies, monopoly newspapers, TV stations, information software, fiber optics, cable television, and cellular telephones. Today we have, among other such areas, entertainment software, wireless communications, multimedia companies, CASE software, RISC microprocessors, computer networks, and aspects of biogenetics. To identify such industries does not call for an MBA or skill in higher math. It does require an awareness of current trends. *You buy a few leaders in each sector, and stay with the most successful.* As long as you are disciplined about the price you pay, and what you continue to hold, you will prosper. You float along in a rapidly flowing river. With luck you hit on a company or two that changes the world.

Great specialty companies: A specialty company does something superlatively well; that is, it has an extremely strong "business franchise." Sometimes, indeed, a company in a dull industry is so outstandingly successful as to constitute a subindustry in itself. Take UST, formerly U.S. Tobacco, the leading maker of moist snuff.* I described it in my *Forbes* column, then in my first book, fifteen years ago, and many times since. It has steadily risen through the entire period. Warren Buffett bought in not long ago. Tobacco is a no-growth industry domestically, but moist snuff, which in essence is very finely cut chew-

---

* When I first wrote about the company in *Forbes*, I called the average person's reaction to this idea "the ha-ha effect." It's a good sign when people are surprised by the conception behind an investment.

ing tobacco, is a growth sector on its own. After the famous Surgeon General's Report in 1964, cigarette advertising was banned from television, and UST's Copenhagen and Skoal brands were among the few tobacco products that could still be sold on TV. The company exploited this advantage—an example of what might be called "mandated prosperity"—and its growth surged. Because of moist snuff's short shelf life before it turns dry, UST enjoys a quasi-monopoly. A potential competitor can't afford to put out and take back all the unsold tins. UST's return on equity runs over 50 percent—the highest in the whole food, drink, and tobacco industry. In a similar kind of catbird seat are Great Lakes Chemical, the dominant producer of bromine; State Street Bank of Boston, the leading custodian of international mutual funds; and Schlumberger, which does most of the world's wireline testing of what's down the hole in oil wells. All these companies almost *are* their industry. Not infrequently, *a growth company creates its own market.*

Often an outstanding company in a dull industry is a safer bet than one in a hot but highly competitive industry. You tend to see dull managers in a dull industry, so the tigers in an outstanding company in such an industry are more likely to have things their way. Watch out that your growth stock doesn't require endlessly more cash to keep up with its market, which can turn it into a Ponzi scheme. The leading bank in a primary growth area is quite likely to run short of capital itself, besides being drawn into wormy loans. The number three bank in a dull territory is often preferable.

Buying

Determining the right price for a growth stock is no easy matter. When the price is low, one tends not to believe that the growth is really there. Then, when the company has proved its merit, the stock is likely to become overvalued. One surprisingly helpful rule of thumb is that *the stock's price-earnings ratio should not exceed the sustainable percentage growth rate,* and preferably be less. In other words, a 15 percent growth rate justifies fifteen times earnings. The useful rules worked out by T. Rowe Price, the father of this investment style, are set out at length in my book *The Money Masters* (1980). One is to *establish a target price-earnings ratio around one-third over the lowest p/e of recent market cycles.* I find that looking at a long chart of a company's earnings, dividends, and stock prices is indispensable, and prefer those put out by Securities Research (101 Prescott Street, Wellesley Hills, MA 02181-

UST INC. (UST)

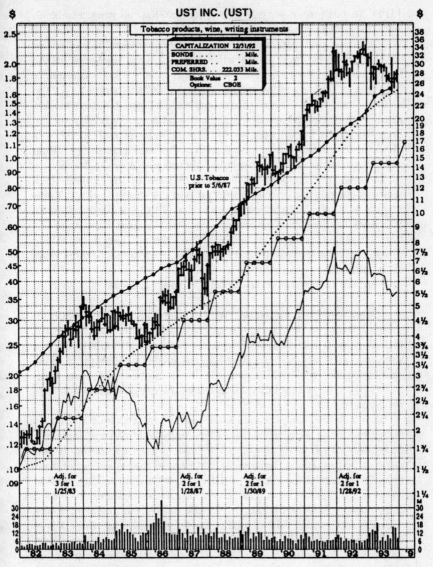

Tobacco products, wine, writing instruments

CAPITALIZATION 12/31/92
BONDS . . . . . · Mil.
PREFERRED . . · Mil.
COM. SHRS. . . 222.033 Mil.
Book Value · 2
Options: CBOE

U.S. Tobacco
prior to 5/6/87

Adj. for
3 for 1
1/25/83

Adj. for
2 for 1
1/28/87

Adj. for
2 for 1
1/30/89

Adj. for
2 for 1
1/28/92

Source: Securities Research, Inc.

3319). You can often see just by inspection what has proved to be an attractive price-earnings ratio.

If you are able, you should do a *discounted internal rate of return calculation*. In essence, you plot the earnings out a few years, on the assumption that the growth rate will in time taper off to the economy's overall rate: "regress to the mean." Then you ask the computer for the discount rate that will reduce that stream of earnings to today's market price. With a few adjustments, that gives you the rate of return you can hope to receive. I greatly prefer this approach, for growth stocks, to a dividend discount model, since growth companies have such exciting uses for their cash that they should only pay very low dividends.

A convenient measure of the attractiveness of the growth stock sector is the relative price-earnings ratio of the stocks in the T. Rowe Price New Horizons Fund compared to that of the Standard and Poor's 500 Stock Average. (See the chart on the New Horizons Fund on p. 13.) Very roughly, this oscillates between one time and two times, taking three years or so to make its journey, and pausing for about three years at the bottom.

Here are two useful ways of thinking about growth:

1. *Downstream Beneficiaries*. Who gained from inventing the automobile? Over the decades, most of the manufacturers went bust. It took dozens of bankrupt American car companies to create the few surviving ones, which themselves are only mediocre businesses. However, suburban real estate, shopping malls, motels, and other businesses based on the mobility conferred by the car have been immense beneficiaries.

Similarly, the computer chip has resulted in ferocious and costly struggles among the original innovators, both American and Japanese. Many of them had to abandon the field. But as computation gets cheaper by the second, businesses that need to manipulate enormous volumes of data thrive. Some of the examples are surprising, such as the *Reader's Digest*. The magazine is of course the most famous part of the company, but the big money is made by the retailing arm: books, records, and the like. The company has tens of millions of families in its database, which is adjusted each time a customer makes a purchase, so it learns how to send out mail solicitations more and more efficiently. And the software end of the business, which arose because the computer existed, is often more profitable than the computers themselves. Electronic Data Systems (EDS), which made H. Ross Perot his billion, doesn't make computers, but has a better return on capital

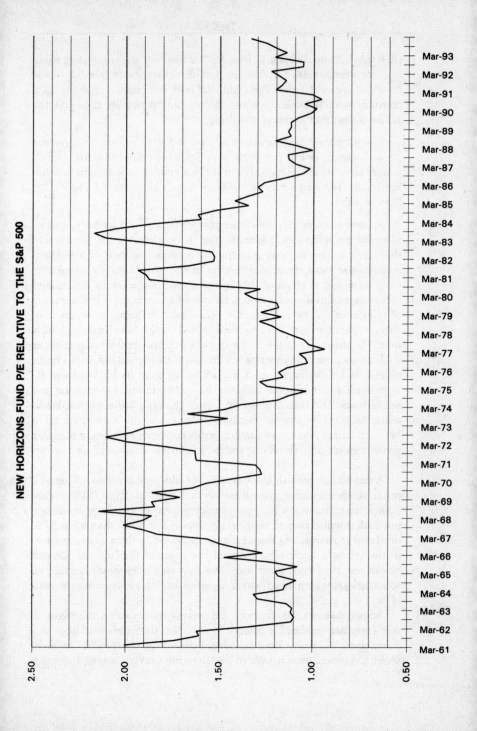

NEW HORIZONS FUND P/E RELATIVE TO THE S&P 500

than most of the companies that do: It takes over the computing function for companies, and handles health insurance claims for whole
states. Huge cables pipe data from all over the country into the EDS
complex outside Dallas, where the company processes it to give the
answers that management requires.

2. *Upstream Beneficiaries.* When an industry grows, its suppliers
grow. Sometimes one company supplies a particular raw material or
widget to most of the manufacturers in a growth industry. In a building boom, Tecumseh Products, which makes heat controls, will infallibly prosper.

3. *Downstream Victims.* The automobile also did its bit to under-
mine values in the clogged inner cities by making it easier to escape to
the suburbs. Investors admire the phenomenal success of Wal-Mart,
perhaps the most successful retailer in the world, but do not always
think of the fatal effect of this company and its peers on the smaller
stores that cannot match its efficiencies of scale. Similar is the impact
of television on the print media. Railroads, by bringing cheap mid-
western produce to eastern markets, killed off the New England family
farm. A curious example is the impact of antidepressants and other
such drugs on mental hospitals. One can treat mental afflictions more
efficiently by dosing the patients with pills than by having them lie
around all day in hospital beds, so the former inmates are turned into
outpatients. And consider the impact of the fax on the telegraph and
telex. As soon as the fax became widespread, the message part of
Western Union became virtually worthless. So my point is, in studying
growth, don't only think out the beneficiaries, think out the victims.

A dangerous growth stock trap is the old-time favorite selling at a
premium price whose growth has in fact faltered. Even if the dream
comes true, the stock may not perform, and if investors are disappointed, it will collapse. There are probably not more than a few hundred real growth stocks that can be understood by the average investor
in the whole economy, so many if not most of the "official" growth
stocks are dangerous imitations. Most growth stock funds contain all
too many great former growth companies, or companies whose growth
is only a hope.

Sometimes, on the contrary, a company that is still a valid growth
stock has been so beaten down in the market that it also qualifies as a
value stock. A growth stock that had been wildly overpriced can be so
badly punctured that it falls to less than net current assets. In such a

INTERNATIONAL BUSINESS MACHINES CORP. (IBM)
"IBM can only go up": The fall from grace of a "Religion Stock."

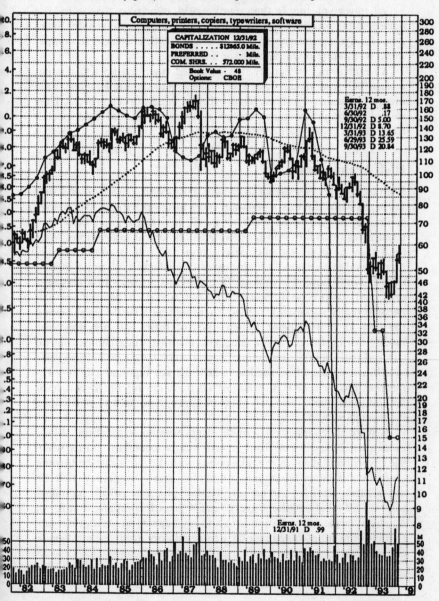

Source: Securities Research, Inc.

case the downside risk is minor, while the upside possibilities remain intact.

Whatever you buy in the growth world, remember that in today's environment you have to be a world-class company to be safe. Every great foreign company wants to establish a U.S. presence, so competition from abroad will appear soon enough.

An exception is what are usually called emerging growth companies, which may or may not ever make it into the big leagues. Most investors should own some, to stay abreast of new developments. They should be bought through a broker or advisor or mutual fund specializing in this class of enterprise.

High Technology

High technology is a subset of growth, but one that has its own rules. To begin with, there is a separate cycle in the pricing of technology stocks, as shown in the chart on p. 17. It is not a good idea for a retail investor to buy into promising technological innovations. Wait until they have proven themselves, and particularly until management has demonstrated a high degree of *business* skill, not a quality usually found among inventors. Of a dozen companies in a very new area, perhaps two or three will work out, and perhaps only one will become really successful. Indeed, there will be a battle royal among the new entrants, during which most of them will not only lose money but be forced out of business. High-tech companies that do succeed require huge amounts of capital, which may be hard to raise in difficult times. Often the losers lack the key ingredient in any enterprise: *business* skill. For almost all investors high-tech is a hard area to understand, and it is thus an appropriate area to participate in through a fund.

Beware the impact on growth of government regulation. Whole industries regularly fall from growth status to dullard status when the government decides to make points with the electorate by turning them into villains: telephone companies, steel companies, defense companies, electric companies, banks, pharmaceutical manufacturers . . . the list lengthens every year. A growth company that is not a natural target of regulation is in a vastly happier situation than one that is being subpoenaed regularly by regulatory agencies and Senate committees.

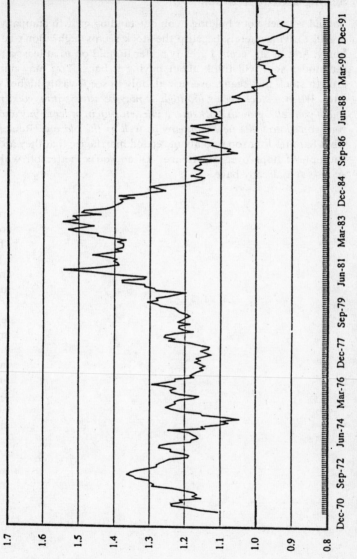

TECHNOLOGY RELATIVE PRICE/EARNINGS*

March 31, 1992

* Equally weighted composite of over 300 technology companies.
Source: Morgan Stanley Research.

Selling a Growth Stock

Should you sell your holding in an outstanding growth company that is still thriving merely because the stock seems high? Don't be in a hurry. And in any event I greatly prefer to hold on to at least a token remainder so I will think about buying it back. You may dump a growth stock that seems overpriced, only to see it vastly higher years later. *When a stock seems too high, it may be anticipating good news. And if you sell a growth stock after a price run-up in order to buy another, you won't know the new company as well as the old one.* Remember what Samuel Johnson said about second marriages, that they are "the triumph of hope over experience." Often you're better off with the spouse you already have.

Value Investing: The Pawnshop

The value investor, or bargain hunter, tries to buy a dollar for fifty cents, over and over again. That's easier than it sounds. At any time many companies are selling in the market far below their own breakup value—what the underlying assets could be liquidated for. And occasionally stocks are available for substantially less than the investor's share of the company's net quick assets—essentially, the cash in the bank, net of debt, with the business itself thrown in for nothing.

In rockbottom bargain investing, how well a company's business is going can often be ignored, since one way to get full value for your stock is through the sale of the whole affair, and the worse things are, the sooner that may be.

In any event, the tests for a bargain issue are essentially filters. Here are some famous ones tested by Benjamin Graham, considered the father of systematic security analysis:

Tests for Bargain Issues

1. Buy a stock for no more than two-thirds of its net quick assets, giving no value to the plant or goodwill.

2. Buy when a stock's "earnings yield" (the reciprocal of the price-earnings ratio) is twice the AAA bond yield, or when its dividend value is two-thirds of the AAA bond yield—in both cases on condition that the company owes less than it's worth.

3. Buy stock in a company with enough in assets so that a bank would lend it an amount equal to its stock market capitalization. (This used to be a somewhat exotic test, but then became crazily overworked during the leveraged buyout vogue.)

When should you sell? Graham's answer was, when a stock becomes 50 percent overvalued on the basis of the rules used for buying it, either because its earnings have fallen or because its price has risen.

A handy compilation of such rules for buying and selling bargain issues can be found in Graham's *The Intelligent Investor*, or indeed in my summary of Graham in *The Money Masters*. It's hard to lose money with this technique. The procedure is essentially a series of formulas for quantifying selectivity. If you are a tough enough buyer and a disciplined seller, you will do well. Over long periods, tests 1 and 2 above, rigorously applied, have given an annual return on investment of about 18 percent compounded.

But if you're so selective, will you be able to buy anything at all? Often, yes, but not always, and not necessarily in large amounts. So the bargain-issue hunter should expect to divide his portfolio among dozens of different stocks. That procedure will have the further advantage of not making him too nervous about them, even though any one could make him queasy, since rockbottom bargains are often found in unsuccessful or even failing companies. If the market is so high that very few stocks qualify, then probably the best course is to step aside and wait for the next bear market. There's always another one coming along. Or you can look for good buys in the growth or emerging market sectors, if they are reasonably priced at the time.

A familiar business is conducted along exactly these lines: the pawnshop. Few objects accepted by the pawnbroker would excite the eye of a collector. Yet a well-run pawnshop almost never loses money. Every object is taken in at a price well below what the pawnbroker, as a matter of close experience, knows he can sell it for. So, if the investor spreads his money around in a pawnbroking spirit, the results will be dull but sure. Graham called this philosophy insisting on a "margin of safety," and I think that describes it very well.

Investors who have followed this approach over long periods find that the average turnover period of each holding is about four years. Lots of bargains come in during bear markets, and can be sold at a nice profit in the ensuing bull market. Treasure chests with the value of the contents written on the outside of the box, however faintly, or at least

THE PRICE/REPLACEMENT COST RATIO

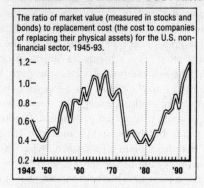

The ratio of market value (measured in stocks and bonds) to replacement cost (the cost to companies of replacing their physical assets) for the U.S. non-financial sector, 1945-93.

Source: James Tobin in *Wall Street Journal*, November 20, 1993.

whose contents can be detected by X-rays, do not remain unrecognized forever.

Value investing, the basic approach until about 1950, once referred primarily to the appraised worth of the company's physical assets, which might add up to more than its market capitalization. Today, professional investors, such as Warren Buffett, may look to the *present value of the company's future stream of earnings.* Obviously harder than totting up the machine tools and real estate. By the same token, though, if the pro gets it right, he has less competition in buying.

From time to time stocks get either too high or too low compared to the private-market value or the replacement cost of the same companies. When they are too high, you will see a rising torrent of public issues as the companies rush to capitalize on a chance to sell stock for more than management thinks it's worth.* When, on the contrary, companies are selling in the stock market for much less than they are worth to private buyers, then they bid for their own stock in the market or are bought out by their management and private investors. During these periods funds or investors specializing in takeovers do splendidly.

I am, incidentally, cool to such takeovers as a matter of public policy, for two reasons: First, they keep managers worried about their stock price, making their orientation even more short term. Second, if

---

* This was the situation early in 1994.

investors ignore short- and medium-term fluctuations, they can ride the long-term upward trend of equity prices. If, however, they are spooked out of a holding by a bid coming off a market bottom, they are out of the game for good, and don't participate in the long-term rise. Manipulators, buttressed by an insincere "fairness opinion" from a pliable investment banker, often take over a company for a quarter or less of what they resell it to the public for a few years later. Sometimes they get the company for nothing except their own "fees." I have often been taken out of a stock I liked in a poor market by such a bid above the then market price, but have always wished it hadn't happened. I don't care about the short or medium term. What difference does it make? Should you worry about the market value of your house if you aren't a seller? I care a lot, though, about missing a rise that goes on for years and years thereafter.

Today, one can add foreign exotica to the catalogue of specialties within the value category. When a market category becomes too popular, sooner or later it will fall too far, abroad as domestically. An example is Latin American debt. After the petrodollar-recycling fiasco and the bankruptcy of many Latin American issuers, most investors abandoned the whole subject. And yet, with the overthrow of many Latino dictators, whose étatist doctrines were mostly an excuse for graft, new hope has come to many countries. But not all at once. So first one and then another becomes a satisfactory credit risk. Guided by an adroit operator, such as Deltec in New York, one can scout around those countries and prosper admirably, as long as one doesn't linger too long.

A variation that is deservedly rising in popularity is overseas small companies. They have been neglected by the U.S. analytical fraternity. Two excellent firms, Ralph Wanger's Acorn, and Tweedy, Browne, among others, have started funds in this category, and others will doubtless follow.

Distressed Securities

Within the value category lies a major subsection, which nonprofessional investors usually avoid, namely, companies emerging from bankruptcy; out-of-favor bonds with interesting assets behind them; companies whose stocks do not yet reflect proposed mergers (risk arbitrage); and the like. However, in value investing, you compare your appraisal for a company with its market capitalization. So you will analyze its different classes of securities. After all, if the stock is interesting, the senior issues, which are safer, must be considered too. Thus, good value investors often deal in merger arbitrage, deflated convertibles, and the like.

Observing what actually works, I find that this area is one of the safest and most consistently profitable for those who can operate in it competently, in part because of the lack of competition from retail investors. Incidentally, you should always take careful note of the market price of the bonds of a company you are interested in. Since the bond market is dominated by highly informed professionals who are in a position to follow developments closely and act ahead of the public, rising or falling bond prices are a clue to what the best-informed observers think about a company.

Bear Baiting

The safe time to invest is when there's "blood in the streets," as the adage goes,* and the dangerous one is when everything looks wonderful. That has to be so in a market situation. If all the children sit on the south end of the seesaw because that's the end that's going up, it can't go up. If the outlook is so bright that "everybody" is fully invested, where will the new buying come from to put the market still higher? Quite the contrary: The market will probably decline, even if the good news is true.

The principle of contrarianism applies not only to the market as a whole but to major sectors, such as the growth stocks. It is best to buy growth stocks when the market is skeptical of them, and doesn't give them as high a price-earnings premium over the Dow as they deserve.

The Unpopularity Contest

In a similar way, from time to time particular categories of assets fall into such disrepute that most investors won't touch them. Often they are the discredited former favorites of aggressive banks in the previous expansion phase. Office buildings and farmland seem to qualify today: The banks and savings and loans are still dumping them on a firesale basis, regardless of long-term values. A few years ago it was LBO debt,

---

* Often ascribed to that shadowy figure "Baron Rothschild." There have been scores of Barons Rothschild, in Paris, London, and Vienna, among other places. Maybe they're repeating this utterance generation after generation, or maybe it was actually first said by Nebuchadnezzar. In French you say, *Achetez aux canons, vendez aux clairons:* "Buy on the cannons; sell on the trumpets": i.e., buy during a siege and sell when it's lifted.

and before that, Latin American paper. Before that it was oil tankers, some of whose maiden voyages were directly from the shipyards to the scrap heap. Passive investors should not dabble in these exotica directly. Wall Street firms create pools to "securitize" them, and if you know what you are doing, you can find remarkable opportunities.

You can do very well in the market just buying stocks that are out of vogue. The problem is to systematize this procedure. One formula that has worked well is just buying the ten highest-yielding Dow industrials. The presumption is that if they have dropped enough so that their yield is up, it's because their popularity is too far down, and will rise when the fit passes. Over the twenty years ended December 1993, this approach returned 16.4 percent compounded, compared to 11.3 percent for the Dow. It even gave a small profit in the ghastly bear market of 1973–74. It also works in foreign markets. The point is that things are rarely as bad as they seem, in part because if things go badly, a great company will usually pull up its socks: shuffle managers, restructure, get reenergized.

Going into 1994, this method would have suggested holding (in order of high yield) Woolworth, Texaco, Philip Morris, Exxon, J. P. Morgan, Eastman Kodak, Merck, Du Pont, Chevron, and Union Carbide.

Emerging Markets

There are a number of additional techniques that a bold and well-informed investor can try. One I think highly of is buying stocks of good companies in misunderstood or overlooked countries, usually in the "emerging" category.*

Several developments have made the emerging markets particularly interesting in recent years. First, the discrediting of communism has freed many countries from the shackles of oppressive and often corrupt socialist regimes. The handful of demented survivors, notably North Korea and Cuba, are scarcely advertisements for the old ways. Privatization and deregulation are gaining worldwide. Most Asian and Latin American economies are booming, and many in Eastern Europe and Africa are doing well. With 6 percent of the world's stock market capitalization, emerging markets represent only 1 percent of global investment portfolios. And although they have 80 percent of the world's population, the emerging countries consume only 25 percent of world output. A United Nations study predicts that this could more than double in two generations. If so, some countries will enjoy fabulous growth rates, which well-situated companies in those countries will more than share. You can see it happening already.

Back in the 1950s Mexico, for instance, was considered a fine place

* I am a director of four emerging market mutual funds: One tripled in its first two years; another rose 86 percent in 1993. One has to recognize that advances on this order suggest that a correction must be coming.

for business, but by the late 1970s, after years of misrule by corrupt insiders, most investors had given up. When President Salinas finally swept out the "dinosaurs" and installed young ministers dedicated to free enterprise, investors for a long time couldn't believe it. By the time they finally did, the market had boomed, and it has risen dozens of times since.

The economic stabilization and recovery of Chile under the harsh rule of General Pinochet is a somewhat similar story. I spotted Chile as a turnaround when Pinochet stepped down, and became a director of the first European-based Chile fund. I remember visiting La Andina, the Coca-Cola bottler in Santiago. The plant functioned smoothly, management was alert, and the market was growing rapidly. Outside investors didn't yet believe in Chile, though, so the stock was languishing at far below the plant's replacement value. We bought a good position in the fund. In the next years it rose thirty-fold! The Chile story is being echoed in Argentina and Brazil. The astonishing booms in such Asian areas as Hong Kong, Singapore, Korea, Thailand, and Taiwan are of course familiar; India, Indonesia, Sri Lanka, Vietnam, and parts of Africa may well follow.

There are always some markets that are emerging: Not long ago even the major foreign markets were in general neglected here. Today, that's over. So although there are often particular opportunities in developed foreign markets, because they are less efficiently covered by analysts than ours is, "abroad" no longer sells more cheaply per se than the United States, only whatever is "emerging" at the time.

An interesting advantage of emerging markets is that some of them seem to have low correlations with the U.S. market, ranging from negative correlations for Argentina, Pakistan, India, and Venezuela to very low positive correlations in, for instance, Chile, Taiwan, Portugal, and Korea. This offers the investor a degree of performance stabilization.

The term *emerging* does not designate an unchanging list of countries in the way that "Islamic" or "Mediterranean" or "Latin American" does. Rather, it means those countries that are catching up at the time. Obviously, communism's collapse and the diffusion of the techniques of higher productivity, together with organized capital markets, create a long list of "emerging" opportunities today. Each country, and the whole category, has ups and downs, so the problem becomes one of selection.

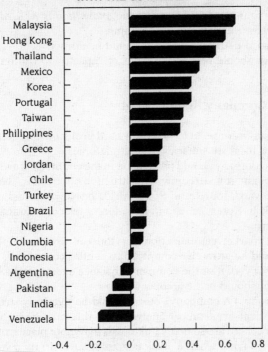

**EMERGING MARKETS CORRELATIONS
WITH THE US MARKET**

Source: Pictet & Cie

Here is a simplified ranking system to help in sorting out emerging
markets. I propose both strategic and tactical criteria.

Strategic Requirements

1. An active stock market.
2. A convertible currency.
3. Political stability, with a commitment to free enterprise and low
   regulation.
4. An educated, industrious, sensible population.
5. A high savings rate.
6. A low level of government spending.

Tactical Requirements

1. The country must be improving, *more than is realized.*
2. Interest rates should be declining.
3. General market valuations should be attractive.
4. There should be slack in industry capacity utilization.

Specific Company Requirements

1. *Management must be honest.* A hard problem! One solution is to favor local subsidiaries of multinationals.
2. The company should participate in the country's growth, such as through infrastructure construction in Chile, banking in Botswana, tourism in South Africa or New Zealand, the China trade in Korea, cement in Ecuador, or telecommunications anywhere.
3. The market capitalization per ton (or whatever) of capacity should be attractive compared to similar countries.
4. The *direction* of the company's balance sheet, particularly as to cash, should be favorable.
5. (Perhaps) A company's stock should be relatively strong. (I am skeptical of technical analysis, but this may be an exception: Since there are so many unknowns in remote places, one may be safer buying when a stock is gaining favor in its own market.)

On the capacity utilization point, it is extraordinary how often analysts compare, let us say, the price-earnings ratio of cement companies in various countries without distinguishing between those that are operating at, for instance, 50 percent and 100 percent of capacity. It makes all the difference! *A company selling at a lower p/e and operating near capacity may be less attractive than one with a higher p/e but operating well below capacity.* Sooner or later economic activity picks up in almost any country. Output and earnings then boom for companies with low capacity utilization rates, and the price-earnings ratios decline.

The analyst should compare industries across countries on a realistic basis, e.g., the market price per ton (or other unit) of installed capacity; the price to net current assets *after all debt* (also called net-net current assets); the price-sales ratio, and the other obvious ratios. You make extraordinary discoveries. For instance, the price per installed hectoliter of Greek breweries when I last looked was a quarter of the price in Chile, and the market capitalization per installed telephone line in Chile was recently four times that of Brazil. You buy oil in Russia for cents a barrel, compared to $7 here, and cement plants for $1 per ton of capacity, compared to $40 in Eastern Europe and $140 here.

The emerging-country investor needs to develop at least one reliable local source of information, and be a competent enough financial analyst to transform the reported figures into more or less real figures. Alternatively, he can deal with an international broker who has these capabilities, or (perhaps best) buy a fund. As usual, he should buy in the midst of bad news, when the market is discouraged, and assets are selling below their replacement cost.*

And remember that an excellent way to play the turnaround in an emerging country is through its bonds, not just its stock. I would stick to sovereign-risk paper, whether international or domestic, rather than getting involved with corporate issues, which are illiquid and hard to analyze. But watch out for this sinister scenario: In some countries, the ministers who hand out public works contracts collect huge kickbacks. When the next revolution comes along (and in the Third World you must expect revolutions), they go to jail, and their proceedings are scrutinized by a hostile commission. If the ministry issued bonds to pay for construction projects, the payments on those bonds—including bonds held abroad—may be held up while the new government figures out how much of the issue went for real production and how much represents graft.

A wonderful time to enter an emerging market is when the government decides to let local pension funds invest in equities. This often coincides with major privatizing: To get an airline or port off their hands, the authorities have to create a demand for its securities. Thus, everything happens at once.

---

* In 1992 the economy and the stock market in that fortunate country, New Zealand, were so depressed that some listed farming companies were selling for even less than their cash in the bank, with the farm and livestock free. Nobody would touch the place. Jim Rogers came back and proclaimed that he was buying. Two years later many farming stocks had doubled, and I read in today's *Southland Times* (February 4, 1994), "Southland investors are rushing . . . sharebrokers to take advantage of the strong sharemarket. Business for city sharebrokers has in some cases more than trebled this year as . . . newcomers join the queues to increase earnings on their money. . . . Overseas money coming into New Zealand is leading the surge."

Reverse Engineering

This may not endear me to my peers in the investment business, but my advice to most readers is *to start by piggybacking on the thinking of the best professionals*. It will save you a great deal of research time, and time is indeed money. It's like having the answers in front of you when you take a math exam. And unlike an exam, which is to test whether you really can do math, in the investment competition you only need a few answers. Never fear, *the great investors do the same thing*. Almost all have networks, often with formal meetings, where they swap ideas with each other. And they constantly scrutinize each other's moves, using the publicly available techniques I am going to describe.

So how does one go about reverse engineering? The first step is to identify some fund managers whose way of thinking one finds congenial. If you like owning assets at a discount more than trying to prophesy the future, you may not be comfortable in the growth stock world, and should perhaps seek your bargains among the holdings of a few "value" funds instead. And if you find new technologies baffling, so be it—leave them aside. If, on the contrary, you enjoy looking ahead and aren't fond of the idea of owning a collection of cheap but dull companies, then pick and choose among the holdings of growth managers.

A technology or emerging-growth fund is much more likely to give you a good idea for a technology or emerging-growth investment than is a general fund, simply because the manager stands or falls by this one sector, in which he must therefore be well informed. The manager of a general fund will want it to be "represented" in each sector, and may thus choose a large, safe company rather than the smaller, less well known specialty company that is likely to be the big winner and which the specialty manager is specifically paid to find. It's just like dining out: You're more likely to find the best risotto in an Italian restaurant than in a Howard Johnson's.

The periodic "Roundtables" of top investment professionals published in *Barron's* are of the utmost value. Some of the participants spend weeks preparing for these sessions, marshaling their ideas and brushing up on the facts.

You can save time by using services that sum up and to some extent analyze what a number of outstanding funds and investment managers are doing. One is much better off studying the moves of a buy-and-hold manager, such as Bill Ruane of Sequoia Fund, than one who likes rapidly getting in and out. Outstanding Investor Digest, at 14 East 4th Street, New York, NY 10012, publishes a series called *Portfolio Reports* that shows the stocks that a hundred or so superior managers have been buying, and the amounts. Another part of the same service shows which among these managers holds any given security. So if, for instance, you are interested in what Warren Buffett is up to, you can look up Berkshire Hathaway. A while back you could see that he was continuing to buy Wells Fargo, of which Berkshire then owned 6.5 million shares, worth $700 million, or 12 percent of the company. You could then see who else was buying Wells Fargo, and how much they owned. In the issue I have in front of me, Wells Fargo was also bought by an affiliate of Julian Robertson's Tiger Management, another excellent investor. So the indications were favorable. A companion service of the same firm contains interviews with the same managers, and prints extracts from their reports to stockholders. If you liked what you heard, you could call Wells Fargo to ask for information.

A service called 13-D Research, Inc., at Southeast Executive Park, 100 Executive Drive, Brewster, NY 10509, shows which institutions hold interests in companies that have gone above the 5 percent level, and then discusses the companies and the apparent rationale for the purchase. Very helpful!

There are more complete descriptions of mutual fund and investment manager transactions, such as those of Vickers Stock Research Corporation, 226 New York Avenue, Huntington, NY 11743. Morningstar Inc., of 53 W. Jackson Boulevard, Chicago, IL 60604, gives excellent descriptions of mutual funds and their holdings. However, there are enough ideas in the *Outstanding Investor* series to give the reverse-engineering practitioner as much as he needs to chew on. In fact, you should hold down the number of managers you study, and be extremely selective about which ideas you pursue. Remember, you only need to find one good stock a year, but you do need to know more about it than most other people. So keep your quest focused!

You never quite know why a manager is making an initial purchase of a stock. If it is in a managed portfolio, the client may have directed the transaction. If it is in a fund, one submanager may be buying without real conviction, and may then turn around and sell again. *So the most meaningful transaction is when an outstanding manager— what I call a "master"—is adding systematically to an already substantial position, with a couple of other masters starting to follow suit.*

On the sell side, one should be *extremely* wary if a manager who has been fond of a stock for years and thus knows it intimately has started to sell it.

If you are going into the reverse-engineering business systematically, you should ask for the reports of the mutual funds you are interested in, or buy a few shares to make things more interesting, and read what the manager says in his reports to shareholders. Some fund managers will send you copies of interviews they give to the financial press, which provide further insights.

As you collect a few dozen highly promising stocks in this way, you should see what *Value Line* has to say about them. How are the sales progressing, how are the profit margins and return on capital holding up, is the research and development budget being sustained, and so forth. If you like what you find, you should send to the companies for the published material, notably the annual and quarterly reports and the 10K and 10Q, and do further analysis. *I suggest asking the shareholder relations representative, among your other questions, which press or other reports he thinks highly of.* Here are two hints on that subject. First, if it turns out that there has been little or no Wall Street research put out on the company recently, *that's a good sign,* not a bad one. It's much better if the stock is overlooked when you buy it, and discovery only comes later.* Second, *ask which broker seems to have the best understanding of the company.* Sometimes it will be a nearby regional firm, little known to Wall Street, that follows the company because it's right under its nose. Eventually it gets to know the situation and the

---

* You're particularly safe if people don't know how to pronounce the company's name. When I first recommended the Harte-Hanks monopoly newspaper chain in *Forbes* (after which it went up 1,000%), it was usually pronounced "Hearty-Hanks," so I called this the Hearty-Hanks Syndrome. Schering-Plough is another example: In the old days before it was understood, Schering-Plough used to rise in sympathy when International Harvester advanced on good news.

people intimately. Make contact with that firm and ask people's opinion. Buy a few shares through them to get their attention. They will be in a far better position to give you information on their corporate neighbor, whose managers they know personally, than will a big firm far away.

What if the company won't give you any more than the bare minimum of required information? My suggestion is that you just move on. One objective of the reverse-engineering exercise is to save time, so that you can identify promising targets as quickly as possible. If you encounter unexpected obstacles, why not proceed to an easier objective? There are other fish in the sea. And good companies are usually eager to oblige analysts: They *want* to be understood.

At the end of this entire process you will have winowed down from the thousands of possible stocks a handful whose logic you understand thus far. Note under each stock what elements you find attractive— who is buying it, what percentage is owned by institutions, and the other major factors in your decision to study it further.

The growth investor who is able to think independently can improve this process by figuring out when a holding has been bought because of an anticipated *change for the better. Catching a change is the most profitable of all investment strategies.* On the other hand, it is also a hard maneuver to execute, and getting it wrong can be costly. There is a big difference between a company that is already successfully doing something new and a company that hopes to succeed in the future: what Wall Street calls a "story" stock, in which even professionals usually lose money.

Reverse engineering works for countries as well as stocks. Let me give you an example. Everybody talks these days about the next Chile or the next Taiwan, the way they used to talk about the next Japan. Which country will it be? Perhaps the greatest living new country picker is James Rogers, George Soros's first partner, and since then an eminent investor for his own account.

A few years ago, after a 65,000-mile trip the length and breadth of the globe, he announced to all who would listen that Peru was a buy. Peru! Almost nobody believed him. What about the Shining Path and the Fujimori coup d'état? It all seemed too much. Well, the whole Peru market promptly tripled. The hazards were already reflected in the prices.

Rogers then opined that Botswana looked good to him, and that he had bought all eleven stocks on the local stock exchange. Botswana! Not everybody's first choice . . . one could almost say not *anybody's* first choice. Anyway, finding myself in Gabarone, the capital, some time later I visited the local stockbroker—there's only one—and asked him to tell me the story. He was delighted. It all seems perfectly true. Botswana (the former Bechuanaland) is a remarkably prosperous country, thanks to its vast diamond mines, and having only one dominant tribe, enjoys political stability. It has a government surplus, a trade surplus, and an investment surplus. Hard to find! Furthermore, if tranquility comes to South Africa, Botswana—as its neighbor and trading partner—should do even better than it has already. And the point is that thanks to Rogers I got the story quite a lot more easily than by traveling his 65,000 miles. Indeed, thanks to his hint, I could have done the job over the telephone. His latest wizard wheeze is Iran. It seems that the ayatollahs have at last got the same word as everyone else, namely, that free enterprise and capital markets are the best way out of poverty. Still . . . Iran!

You can also do all this by looking at the transactions in the best international funds, noting the countries they are going into, and then figuring out why. Apply the "emerging-markets" checklists on pp. 27–28. Sometimes the fund manager will tell you, if you ask, even if he doesn't explain it in his quarterly report.

Advice and Advisors

A central decision every investor should face is whether he really expects to succeed in the stock-picking competition, even with "reverse engineering," or whether he prefers to delegate the deciding process to others—for example, by investing in mutual funds or hedge funds, or by relying on an investment counsel firm, or by following the exhortations of one or more investment letters, or getting suggestions from his stockbroker.

Finding a Good Mutual Fund

Few funds beat the averages, and most fund *investors* do worse than the funds, by switching into exciting ideas nearer the end of a run than the beginning. Therefore, a key rule is: *Don't go head over heels into funds that have been hot recently because their area of concentration has boomed.* This tactic performs significantly worse than the market. Market booms rarely last more than two years, and three years is an aging boom.* So don't plunge into Argentina just after the *bolsa* there has quadrupled (as it did in 1991), or into a biogenetics fund after that whole category has just exploded, or into frothy speculations at the top of a bull market.

Instead, buy funds in areas of perennial interest, or flexible funds that move around from sector to sector, perhaps within a broader area.

---

* In the potato business, one says that you don't have three years of good prices in a row, because by the third year, "they plant the sidewalks."

For instance, an emerging-market fund that changes its focus as countries emerge into the limelight and then retreat can be a good idea, particularly if the selection is based on where the best values are found, rather than on flair. Similarly, a technology fund that does not focus on just one sector makes excellent sense, since very few individual investors are in a position to understand technology; or an emerging-growth stock fund.

A fund that has delivered good performance year in and year out in all sorts of markets for a considerable time is much more reassuring than one that zooms from time to time and then crashes. Make sure it's still run by the same manager that was responsible for the good record. The *Forbes* Magazine annual fund issue does an outstanding job rating the funds. I would limit my choices to funds that ranked A or B in both bull markets and bear markets, and particularly those on its Honor Roll. A service called Fidelity Monitor, P.O. Box 124, Rocklin, CA 95677-0124, has outperformed the averages by selecting among the Fidelity family of funds. *But don't switch funds frequently.*

There's no point in buying a fund that is burdened by a sales charge or "load," and these days one should be careful that the fund does not pay the managers either a special fee to push sales or an "exit" fee. In other words, the *total* costs should be added up. Other things being equal, low turnover is of course preferable to a high turnover. Funds run by brokers should, in my opinion, usually be avoided, since they tend to have much higher turnover than funds run by investment counsel firms or professional fund managers with no interest in brokerage. These days, to be sure, the Securities and Exchange Commission (SEC) is tough on mutual fund managers who fail to demand favorable brokerage commission rates for their funds, so there is less to fear than there used to be.

Index Funds

Few investors succeed in beating the averages. But it does not necessarily follow that they should buy index funds, which have their own costs and an arbitrary makeup. There is nothing magic about the Standard and Poor's 500 average, so why try to replicate it, rather than a growth average or a global average? Furthermore, as more managers buy funds indexed to a particular average, the stocks that make up that

---

* As a curiosity, I might mention the Steadman family of funds, which has four members. All four are found in the bottom eight funds for the ten-year performance period ended December 31, 1993.

average become more expensive, and thus less attractive to own, than similar stocks not in the average. The easiest way to achieve superior performance remains the traditional one of holding a diversified list of companies and keeping transactions to an absolute minimum. That way, you directly receive the benefit of the earnings of the companies you own. Any other solution creates an additional level of overhead that can only be justified if the results are superior, which an index fund doesn't try to be. If you want one anyway, the Vanguard Total Stock Market Portfolio (which includes small stocks) is very efficiently run.

Hedge Funds

Hedge funds are still funds, usually in limited partnership form, that charge a percentage profit participation on top of a flat percentage. *It's not worth paying the extra percentage unless the fund really does make use of the flexibility that is available to it* (that is, to use leverage and change from net long to net short) *and does it successfully.*

For a hedge fund to seek a percentage of the net gain on top of a fee is quite reasonable, incidentally. If a fund is long and short on margin, it may be managing two or more times its own equity, so the fee is less than it seems. And the difficulty of this sort of maneuvering makes it an active business, rather than passive investing, justifying a business compensation.

Some hedge funds charge you a percentage of the gain every year, even if the fund is only recovering from an earlier decline. That's silly. You should insist on the "high-watermark" principle: that the percentage applies only to the *net* gain, after you've recovered from earlier losses.

Some hedge funds, such as those run by Julian Robertson and Michael Steinhardt, or (for overseas investors) George Soros, have produced outstanding results over many years, and have a place in the portfolios of large investors. They perform stunts that are beyond the reach of conventional investors, such as making large long and short bets on foreign bond movements using borrowed money. The "securitization" of innumerable financial concepts and the depth of the derivative markets have given these operators a big enough lake to swim in so that they should find plenty to do. *Try to diversify strategies* among hedge funds you own (or keep down covariance, in the Modern Portfolio theory lingo), so that a horrid surprise won't ruin everything. Also, watch out that a successful fund doesn't change its spots as it gets bigger or as its winning strategy attracts imitators. I follow closely about a hundred of them, and find that they are constantly evolving. Short-side hedge funds are the best way to be short without losing sleep, but the most famous short fund operators, the Feshbachs, went net long a year or so ago! *A hedge fund must be run by a master investor to be worth the fees, and a master is by definition flexible.* But his flexibility may lead him into higher risk than you care to assume.

Incidentally, *the multiplication of hedge funds and other unusually aggressive vehicles typifies the final, frothy phase of a bull market.* We are seeing it as I write, in early 1994. During this phase the public—and the professionals who cater to it—is prepared to believe that happy days are here again, that companies' stocks can forever rise faster than their earnings, that margin does not increase risk, and that fund managers can easily be found whose performance will be far superior to other, similar fund managers. In other words, realism yields to the speculative fever.

Investment Advisors

The advantage of an investment advisor (or counsel—same thing) over a fund is that you have someone disinterested to talk to who will *help you shape your strategy according to your circumstances.* He isn't trying to sell you anything.* A good advisor, like a good decorator, assesses your needs, knows the wares that are in the stores, and so can sketch out your realistic alternatives and help you achieve them. There is no guarantee that an investment advisor will improve your performance— although this is certainly to be hoped—but he should increase your investment efficiency and safety. And, if he really knows some good stocks, he can encourage you not to sell just because they have gone up, assuming the values are still attractive, or just because they've gone down.

A professional advisor should have several characteristics: intellectual honesty, realism, a broad experience of life, patience, and outstanding competence in at least one investment approach. *He should derive his satisfaction from helping people, like a teacher, rather than from getting rich himself.* And he should love the investment game. Keen investors often start to get excited when they talk about their

---

* I deplore the tricky use of the word "consultant" by some brokerage firms. Brokers have a commercial, not a professional relationship with the customer, do not have to be disinterested, are not required to know your entire circumstances, and live by selling you things you may or may not need. It is as though a drugstore called itself a clinic.

favorite stocks; their eyes sparkle and they talk more rapidly. Some investment firms provide expertise in such areas as estate planning, insurance, and personal finance generally. Obviously, that can be very helpful. An investment advisor who steers a client into a venture in which he has a separate interest is violating his professional status, and should be viewed with caution, to say the least.

You should visit your advisor every six months or so and talk things over for a couple of hours. You can describe the evolution of your career and family situation, and he can explain his ideas. *Take notes.* He may not bother to initiate such periodic meetings, which are essential to the relationship. Make it clear when you sign up that this is what you expect, and at the end of each meeting set the date for the next one. I suspect it's better to talk in a conference room rather than over lunch: it's easier to take things down, and the atmosphere is more businesslike.

Finding a good advisor requires initiative and common sense, like finding a good doctor. If you are an individual investor, you will want to deal with someone in your own region, or at least in a city where you go frequently. So *the person you want will probably be known to friends of yours.* I would not necessarily give preference to banks or other very large firms; if you do, though, *be sure to get your account into the hands of a top manager: the* top manager, if possible. This takes politics, like wangling a good table in a restaurant. Large institutions usually tend to invest by committee* and to favor immobility, which is easier and more profitable for them; a lively individual is the best counter. By the same token, *in creating a trust, be sure to have a protector, or a committee of adult beneficiaries, who can change the institutional trustee when it gets atherosclerotic.* Without this protection, the family has no leverage in getting its account moved to an able and energetic manager within the institution.

Every superior human institution is inspired by a natural leader who is an outstanding individual. A superior investment firm must *also* have a great investor, usually an odd duck, who should be insulated from daily operations. An investment firm decays when the great leader lets the great investor become swamped by client contacts, selling, or administration. The leader's temptation is to become a public figure. It is better to be a public figure than to run a firm, so when that time

---

* From time to time one is told that "a camel is a horse designed by a committee." The same sages rarely add that a camel is a far more remarkable design achievement than a horse. It can survive frightful heat and drought, as well as sandstorms. Horses are fragile constructions, which faint if you look at them cross-eyed.

comes the leader should turn management over to a new leader. This is often a hard challenge.

Investment Letters

Most subscribers to investment letters fall victim to charlatans. And it almost seems that the services that make the most vehement claims are the most likely to be purveyors of rubbish. Here are some examples, based on twelve-year results, as analyzed by *The Hulbert Guide to Financial Newsletters*. (I am reluctant to use shorter performance periods because of the risk of tagging on to an untested operator or a passing trend.)

The *International Harry Shultz Letter*, published by "chevalier" Harry Shultz, who describes himself as both the most expensive and the most honored of investment swamis, is one of the least useful. According to the Hulbert service, if you followed the chevalier's counsel you would have done about one-eighth as well as the averages over the twelve years ended mid-1992. In that sense he is indeed an expensive advisor.

Joe Granville may be the most famous—or notorious—of all purveyors of investment advice. He engages in fantastic self-promotion displays, and some years ago announced that he never again expected to make a mistaken market call. However, over the same twelve-year period Hulbert calculates that his market letter lost its followers 93 percent of their capital. He also runs a model option portfolio. "On balance," says Hulbert, "it has been a large loser, losing almost everything in 1985, 1986 and 1987. . . . Over the five and one-half years through mid-1992, this portfolio lost 94.7%." (Over the five years through 1987 Granville achieved a loss of 97%, although the distinction becomes somewhat academic.) This is the famous Joe Granville, whose inspirations, once reported on front pages, moved the whole market! Granville advertises that he issued a "buy" signal right after the crash of 1987. His ads fail to add that he also issued one just before the crash.

The *Dines Letter*, put out by self-proclaimed "goldbug" James Dines, has made some disastrous calls on gold. His letter also publishes recommended portfolios. One has done well; several have been abandoned. The average performance has been consistently in the bottom quintile of all letters, with a twelve-year gain of 38.3 percent, about a tenth of the averages.

The *Ruff Times* is another famous purveyor of Wall Street wisdom. Hulbert says: "Overall for the entire 12 years through mid-1992, assuming that Ruff earned the T-bill rate during 1986 when his advice was too vague and incomplete to follow, he underperformed the Wilshire 5000 [average] by a 38.2% to 432.7% margin."

Morningstar, the best-known mutual fund analytical service, now also offers a fund-rating service. Their five-star (highest-ranked) stock funds have fallen far short of the averages, and their bond fund choices likewise.

The *Harry Browne Letter* ranks in the fourth (next to the bottom) quintile over most of the periods Hulbert measures.

Another much-advertised service is *The Professional Tape Reader,* published by Stan Weinstein. As its title implies, it is based on technical analysis, and the results are what you would expect from that approach. Hulbert reports that Weinstein's model stock portfolio gained 48.5 percent for the twelve years through mid-1992, compared to 432.7 percent for the Wilshire 5000.

The *Holt Advisory,* according to Hulbert, provided its followers with a loss of 62.4 percent for the twelve years through mid-1992, compared to a gain of 432.7 percent for the Wilshire 5000.

Financial World publishes several recommended mutual fund portfolios, which the Hulbert service started tracking at the start of 1991. From then to mid-1992, all did much worse than the averages. It also publishes a rating system for stocks. From the start of 1991 to mid-1992, the "A+" stocks did less than half as well as the averages.

These are most of the best-known advisory letters. Some of the others approach black humor. For instance, *Harmonic Research,* which in addition to technical analysis is attuned to "the eclipse cycle and harmonics of the solar year," charged its Futures Portfolio followers $720 per annum to lose 59.1% over the four and a half years ending mid-1992, compared to a gain of 89 percent in the Wilshire 5000, shoving it solidly into the bottom quintile.

Another service, *Your Window into the Future,* offers "Advance Notice of Profitable Moves in Mutual Funds, Precious Metals, Bonds and Options." There is a touch of melancholy in the results. "Portfolio C" lost all its money in both 1988 and 1989, following almost all in 1987. The *Overpriced Stock Service,* itself overpriced at $495 a year, lost 92 percent over its two-and-a-half-year career, compared to a gain of 24 percent for the Wilshire.

*   *   *

Does all this mean that there is not much hope of doing well by following the advice offered by investment newsletters? Correct: very little indeed. What is worse, their advertising is often crazily exaggerated . . . straight from P. T. Barnum. Even the fairer claims may omit such basic considerations as transaction costs, or what happens when all the readers buy or sell at the same time.

Fortunately, *The Hulbert Guide,* a volume of over 500 pages published annually by Dearborn Financial Publishing, Inc. (520 North Dearborn Street, Chicago, Ill 60610-4352), provides a thorough and systematic analysis of newsletter performance. You should certainly study it before subscribing to an investment letter, and *particularly before following a letter's advice.* Hulbert establishes that there are actually only a handful of newsletters which have been going for the full twelve years and have beaten the Wilshire 5000. Here they are: *The Chartist, The Value Line Investment Survey* (and OTC Special Situation Service), and *The Zweig Forecast.* That's the lot!

I have subscribed to many of these services off and on. Besides the basic *Value Line* service, I like to read Richard Russell's *Dow Theory Letter,* P.O. Box 1759, La Jolla, CA 92038, for its many useful insights, and the *Dick Davis Digest,* P.O. Box 350630, Fort Lauderdale, FL 33335, for its notes on what other investors are thinking . . . reverse engineering!

Professionals often read Warren Buffett's annual reports to the shareholders of Berkshire Hathaway, which nonshareholders can obtain by requesting them from the company at 1440 Kiewit Plaza, Omaha, NE 68131. They describe the essence of the businesses Berkshire has interests in, with disarming citations from *Peanuts* and Yogi Berra.

How to Buy a Stock: Cross the River, Groping for the Stones

The big payoff in stock investment is what I call the double play: when a company's earnings grow, and its stock sells in the market for a higher multiple of those higher earnings. To achieve that feat, you need to understand the company, and to get the timing right. The timing, that is, both as to the company's affairs and the stock itself.

Understanding the Company

How do you assemble enough information about a company to buy with confidence, and so that you will be comfortable when the price drops sharply, which sooner or later it will? The answer is, you must know most of the facts that are generally available. The key to great investment success is knowing more than almost anybody else. Quite often you learn in stages. When I entered Wall Street, new employees of investment firms did industry "spreadsheets" by hand, dozens of them, even hundreds. These involved going through the annual reports and yourself calculating the same types of figures that you find in *Value Line:* depreciation, average age of plants, return on capital, free cash flow, R&D budgets, and the like, for all the companies in, for instance, the automobile business or the building business or the steel business or the oil business. After a few years of this you understood how the different companies built up their reported figures, and you had an excellent feeling for the relative positions of the companies themselves within an industry, and for one industry compared to another industry.

You should do a spreadsheet for each company you own. An admirable specimen spreadsheet, that of James Rogers, is found as Appendix I of *The New Money Masters* (1989). Collecting the facts required for such a spreadsheet will render you more nearly immune to casual advice, an enemy of investment success. To compare a company with others in its industry, one handy guide is the *Forbes* "Annual Report on American Industry" issue, which compares returns on capital, profit margins, sales and earnings growth, and the like.

At some point, if you are a substantial enough investor so that this is appropriate, you should either visit a company you find interesting or else ask your stockbroker or bank to arrange for you to attend the next "dog and pony show" for security analysts that the company is holding in your area. A company will usually make a point of sending people who are known to be good spokespersons to these meetings, so don't let yourself be convinced just by what you hear. That would be like a judge deciding a case based on the pleading of only one side's lawyer. Nevertheless, you can sometimes form useful impressions, and it is interesting to see how very hard questions are fielded.* All serious companies claim to be dedicated to growth, and people-oriented. To check these claims, you can ask in a question-and-answer session about the trend of patents and employee turnover, executive training, and the like, which may not appear in the published material. *You should study a company carefully before talking to management, so that you can dig below the surface.*

As I have mentioned elsewhere, it pays to ask the shareholder relations representative or the treasurer *which brokerage house seems to understand his company best.*† You can then request that broker's reports on the company with more confidence than usual. *You must also talk to him in person, though.* He may tell you things that he won't want to write. Brokers often earn more from bonuses than from their salaries, and the bonuses are often linked to the investment banking business they bring in. So, for fear of alienating a corporate client of the firm, or at least of drying up their information source, they are reluctant to be too negative in print.

Establish that the *management is honest* (which is widely known) and *owns a lot of stock. Insider buying is a very good sign.* Management's failure to own a significant stock position constitutes a warning

* I greatly prefer a CEO who talks (and, in the annual report, writes) carefully and cautiously.

† If nobody does, that's okay too. Peter Lynch, the amazing investor who built up the Magellan Fund, describes calling on Volvo, then the greatest Swedish company, and finding that it had not been visited at all by financial analysts. It owned a cash hoard equal to its stock price!

signal about a company. If they don't have faith in it, why should you?

If you want to do a thorough job of studying a company, you should by no means be content with talking to management. You should also talk to some of the company's customers, competitors, and suppliers. This can be fairly easy to do. For instance, if you are thinking of buying stock in a bank, you can ask a few industrial and personal customers how good the service is compared to other banks in the area, and talk to another bank. *A question you should always ask an executive is where would he like to work if he had to go somewhere else, or who the most effective competitors are.* A wonderful source is disgruntled ex-executives: you will pick up rumors and can perhaps spot a few real problems. Another is industry associations. You meet the staff at trade conventions. They hear interesting news, and may enjoy sharing it with someone they consider "folks," perhaps just for the price of a lunch. Finally, *if it is a consumer product, try it out!** You can ask stores you patronize how a company's products compare with the competition's. (In the same spirit, before buying a car I always go to a repair shop and ask about reliability.)

I am often surprised in talking to clients who are businessmen how little use they make of their understanding of their industries. Warren Buffett relates that his father, a life insurance agent, rather than buy stock in his own insurance company, which was selling for three times earnings, or an "earnings yield" of 33 percent, used to put his money into life insurance issued by the same company, on which the investment return was about 2.5 percent.

Often a company executive understands his industry and the companies in it backward and forward, and can employ this knowledge to great effect in placing his own capital.

Good security analysts familiar with business like to look at certain measures of corporate success that are less emphasized than they should be by nonprofessionals.

1. *Return on capital.* This is the ultimate measure of management success. You give your faithful servant one talent and see if he turns it into two or three or four, or loses it. *Capital should include working capital,* since in many companies there is more working capital than fixed capital.

---

* Peter Lynch suggests that the consumer get investment ideas by noticing outstanding consumer products or services. But many attractive products are in such competitive sectors that nobody makes really good money.

2. An interesting variation is the *economic value added*. You derive it by deducting from reported earnings a reasonable approximation of the cost of all the capital tied up in the business. In other words, if a business has $1 billion of total assets, including working capital, on which it makes 11 percent after taxes, and if a reasonable cost of capital is 9 percent, then the real profitability of the business is low. If it makes 15 percent, then the profitability is very satisfactory.

3. Another important business measure is *free cash flow*. Cash flow—earnings before such noncash charges as depreciation—is the financial power of a company: what it can deploy to create new products and develop new markets. If growth is achieved by hocking the company to buy new assets, the investor should be wary. Rather, it should be achieved by directing cash flow not actually needed for depreciation into areas that offer an exceptionally high return on capital.

Here are some more hints:

Keep an eye on the ratio of the company's market capitalization to its revenues, also called *the price-sales ratio*. One times sales is reasonable for a manufacturing company. A wonderful business franchise can sometimes justify as much as three times, but watch out. Companies in emerging markets often sell in the market for as little as a quarter of their own revenues and, rarely, for only a tenth.

Try calculating *the ratio of price to cash flow plus research and development*, particularly in countries where local accounting practices permit manipulation of profit figures more easily than revenues, depreciation, or R&D figures. To give an idea of the difference in the result, here is a leading American and two leading German chemical companies:

	U.S. Company	German Companies	
Ratios	American Cyanamid	BASF	Hoechst
Price/earnings	14.4	13.3	11.4
Price/cash flow + R&D	3.8	2.0	2.0
Price/sales (%)	101.8	30.0	43.9

All of a sudden the German companies look much cheaper than they did on just a p/e basis!

Be sure to determine the consolidated profits of a foreign company. It seems absurd, but for decades analysts included the dividends but *excluded the earnings* of the subsidiaries of Japanese companies in calculating parent company earnings. Consolidating the subsidiaries' earnings often cut the reported p/e in half! And today you can have horrible surprises when you dig into the subsidiaries of, say, Brazilian companies. They may be gravely troubled without this appearing in the parent's accounts, putting the real p/e much higher than it first appears. Understated assets, such as investments in other companies, or fully written-down inventory, can be a bonanza. An example is the immense libraries of old films that slept on the balance sheets of some film studios.

Timing the Right Moment in the Life of the Company

As to positive changes, *one of the few sure things in investment is that the start-up cost of a large new plant creates high depreciation and other charges on earnings that will fall when the plant goes into production. You can thus program an earnings jump.* Analysts spot exciting new products that should boost earnings, but sometimes miss the end of a start-up.

Similarly, a company quite often has to write off the goodwill component of an acquisition—essentially, the business franchise value in excess of the book value—even though the goodwill may be the most interesting part of the acquisition. When the goodwill write-off ends, reported earnings will jump. The same principle holds for heavy research and development expenses required to bring a new product to market. When the expense ends, and the product is released, earnings may soar.

After that, you need to keep an eye on how a new product, or for that matter an old one, is faring. New cosmetics have a cycle, new car models have a cycle, new drugs, new computers, all have a cycle. So one of the central and yet overlooked keys to security analysis is concentrating on company *product cycles* as well as company facts and industry cycles.

Timing a Purchase

The first rule is to *wait until you're sure.* Be fussy. In fact, *good investing is an exercise in controlled fussiness.*

Investment is a "loser's game," like club tennis.* Most points are

* As noted by investment sage Charles Ellis.

lost on errors, rather than won by forcing shots. Since the investor
never has to act, he should focus on not making avoidable mistakes. An
enthusiastic retail investor often pays up for an exciting conception.
Then there is an earnings disappointment, the market becomes disil-
lusioned, and the price drops severely: a double play in reverse, as it
were. Misery! So remember that the safest strategy is being very hard
to please. *Insist on waiting for a stock to satisfy you completely before
you risk your capital.* * All the information you need should be available, and what you learn should satisfy you; that it's a company you
want to be part of. What's the hurry? There are plenty of other possibilities, thousands, in fact. So, take your time.

In value investing, remember that the high rates of return that can
be achieved by that approach *only work if you are rigorous about both
the buying and the selling price,* which between them create your profit
margin, the "margin of safety." You have to turn over your merchandise in a disciplined way.

In growth investing, you have much more leeway on pricing, but
you must keep checking the facts. Begin with a small position and keep
learning as you build up your holding. If things deteriorate, don't linger. Remember, *there are far more ways to lose than to win, and what
you don't own can't hurt you.*

Yet another reason to wait until you feel very comfortable about a
company is that this means that you will have fewer ideas. *You are
safer having a few big, powerful conceptions that you follow closely than
a jumble of insignificant ones that soothe you because they are scattered
and thus unimportant.* For superior results, a growth investor should
have not more than a dozen or so big holdings, probably grouped
around three or four important concepts. At one time the "media"
concept rose to as much as 40 percent of some of my firm's portfolios,
consisting chiefly of television stations and monopoly newspapers.
Many holdings advanced ten times or more. We felt perfectly comfortable with them because we understood them and the market didn't. As
the market perception caught up with the reality, we gradually let
them go.

At the end of all this, you should write a tight one-page description
of the company, particularly looking for (*a*) *a false bear story that is
depressing the price, and if possible, (b) a change that will lift the price.*

---

* This rule is for nonprofessional long-term investors. Master speculators often act
on incomplete information, if they think the odds are in their favor. "If you wait till the
smoke clears," they say, "the train will have left the station."

As to the bear story, either investors have not understood what makes the company good, or there is bad news around that is somehow misleading, or there has been a drain on earnings that will soon end.

It's interesting to work out a compelling and reasonably simple hypothesis of how in time the company's fortunes, and its stock, will move upward. This will give you a benchmark against which to measure its progress.

By the time you have completed this job, you should know more about the company than most brokers. So you may be in a position to exchange information with a broker or advisor you find to be knowledgeable, particularly when it is realized that you are not a competitor. Knowledge is not diminished by sharing. If you and I have a dollar and each gives it to the other, we still have one dollar each. But if you and I both have an idea and share it, each of us has two ideas. Brokers understand this very well. Since the procedure that I have described should give you a better idea of a company than many analysts (who must cover a great many companies), you may well find that they will talk frankly to you. You can then hope to enter the charmed circle of those who know most about the particular company in question. At that point you should not be blindsided by good or bad new developments that take the market by surprise.

The investor should spend almost all his time on learning the facts of the company, and little or none getting half-baked advice from people here and there in the securities business or elsewhere—tips. Most investors, of course, do exactly the opposite: They crave action, and shy away from hard intellectual work. So they receive ideas from a broker they happen to be dealing with, and neither determine whether he has truly researched the company nor bother to do it themselves. Following tips is an excuse for not doing thorough research. The Wall Street joke goes that if you get a tip from the president of a company, you'll lose half your money, and if from the chairman, you'll lose all your money. (A carefully developed idea based on analysis of the transactions of one or more great investors is quite another matter, of course: it can be extremely valuable.)

All good investors are contrarians. The obvious is usually discounted in the market, and therefore its opposite offers the best percentage play. So massive philosophical counteropinion can pay off immensely. For instance, near the top of the interest rate boom Kiril Sokoloff and A. Gary Shilling produced a book called *Is Inflation Ending: Are You Ready?* (McGraw-Hill, 1983). At least 99 percent of all investors would have dismissed the anti-inflationary thesis. And yet, buying long bonds at that time was a prodigiously profitable and almost riskless investment strategy.

Anyway, suppose that at the end of a few months you have a list of companies that you have researched in this way, and then buy stock in a few. The job of maintaining your knowledge as news comes out quarter by quarter and year by year is comparatively simple. You will have been sensitized to the trend in profit margins, product cycles, return on capital, earnings per share, and so forth.

If he has bought well, the average investor should not follow his stocks minutely, and certainly not price them day by day. Price jiggles tell you nothing. It is, however, a very good idea to read your companies' quarterly reports, and perhaps write the highlights on a summary sheet you maintain for that company. But to fret constantly about small movements is nervous-making and counterproductive.

The investor who wants to beat the crowd has to see things differently from the crowd: he must look around the next corner, so to speak. That means *constantly thinking about the implications of change*. A successful professional should do this automatically, but the average retail investor looks only for the ABC sequence, without jumping to DEF and indeed XYZ.

One of the greatest dangers to good investing is a rigid mind. You'll infallibly be stuck with yesterday's ideas, but *the old order changes, and we must change with it*. Thus, any successful theme becomes increasingly dangerous. When it is universally accepted, the time has come to look for the next one. An ingenious solution is to sustain two contrary theses at the same time. In fact, only by operating under contrary theses are you likely to shake yourself free of a false trend before it is too late. In the situation I've just described, rather than sell out your stocks or short bonds in order to buy long bonds, you should hold your short bonds and buy a few very long bonds, to test the opposite point of view. It's much easier to start with a small counterintuitive position and build it up if it is successful. The investor is more likely to miss a gradual change than a sudden one. So *one should feel one's way by degrees*. (As the Chinese say, "Cross the river, groping for the stones.") This gets you into the mood of contemplating the contrary thesis and preparing to act on it. Professionals may test a contrarian thesis on a small scale using futures until they see the theme starting to work out.

Different people have different ways of doing things, but for myself, I have generally found advantage in taking small initial positions, and also splitting my bets on a single concept into different components of a package. For instance, suppose you determine that the time has come to buy a high-tech fund (as indeed, as I write, it may), or an emerging market fund, or build a position in the multimedia industry or pharmaceuticals, or whatever. You are puzzled by which choice to make: the big, established company or several smaller, more dynamic, but not yet fully accepted ones? My own preference in such a case would be to place perhaps half in the "senior" fund or stock and half in the "juniors." I often find that while the senior holding does well, one of the juniors is the big winner.* Also, having the junior positions in place marks your interest, and makes it easier to add more later on.

Note that *a good collection of smaller companies is usually more attractive than very big companies.* You can know them better, they are more likely to maintain their dynamism, they can better dominate particular *niches*, they are less vulnerable to regulation and consumerism, and their stock prices are less susceptible to stampedes. Not surprisingly, over long periods the NASDAQ composite index has outperformed the Dow by a considerable margin. So rather than buy a big-name composite company like GE, a mixed grill of dozens or even hundreds of subcompanies—some growing and some not—I prefer to assemble my own portfolio of outstanding smaller companies, all growing vigorously, which seems to be quite a lot safer.

In timing a purchase one of course needs to give some consideration to the overall market, notably to such objective measures as the prevailing dividend rates compared to bond interest, and the price to replacement book ratio of the Dow or S&P stocks. Note that as more and more service companies, which are less dependent on "hard" assets than heavy manufacturing companies, are included in the averages, the Dow book value falls, and thus its price/book ratio rises. Nevertheless, one should be watching that it has not become crazily high.

One should always compare price-earnings ratios with the prevailing bond rate. Obviously, when bonds are yielding 8 percent, stocks in general should not sell at higher than a price-earnings ratio of 12, or an "earnings yield" of 8 percent, since they are intrinsically riskier than bonds. There is no inherent growth in most companies, so the earnings are all there is. The growth comes from reinvested earnings, not increased output from the same factories. In other words, when bonds

---

* A remarkable example was Peter Lynch running the Magellan Fund. "Of the stocks I buy, three months later I'm happy with less than a quarter of them," he told me.

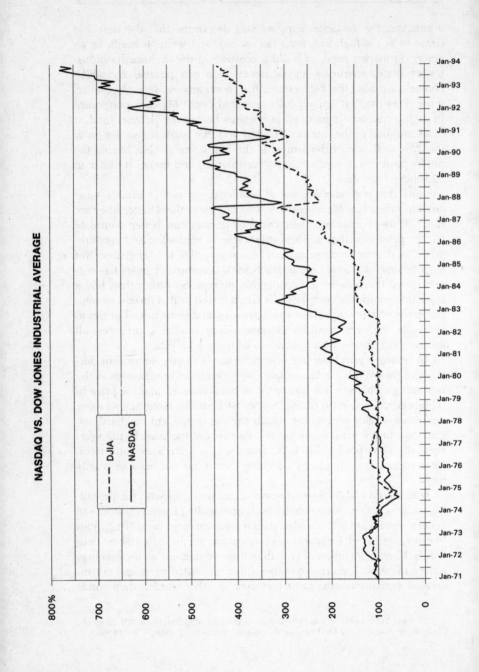

NASDAQ VS. DOW JONES INDUSTRIAL AVERAGE

DJIA
NASDAQ

are yielding 5 percent, a substantially higher p/e is justified* than when they are yielding 10 percent.

The Double Play

Anyway, if everything about a company checks out, and if it is misunderstood in the market for a reason you understand, you may be on the verge of a double play. It works like this: An excellent company is earning $1 a share and selling for $8. You buy the stock, and your hopes are realized. Three years later the company is earning $2 a share. If your original analysis was on target and the improvement is real, then the market should accept the authenticity of the new $2 earnings, and bid the stock up from 8 times $1 earnings to perhaps 12 times $2 earnings—a market price of $24, let us say. So a doubling of the earnings should produce a tripling of the stock price. A few years later still it may be 15 times $4 earnings, or a $60 market price. Professional investors never settle for just a "good stock"; they always look for the double play. If executed with care, this aggressive approach to investing can be safer than buying into big-name companies, where even if you (and everybody else) are right, you won't be properly rewarded.

* Warren Buffett has opined that the Dow is worth twice book if T-bills yield 5 percent, and 1.5 times book if T-bills yield 8.5 percent. Another Wall Street maxim holds that a reasonable p/e for the Dow is 20 minus the inflation rate: the "Rule of Twenty."

When to Sell, or How to Boil a Frog

The investor's first concern must be to survive; that is, not to lose a lot of money. I mean in real terms, not quotational terms. The market rises and sets all the time. Don't worry too much about that. So does the sun. Truly losing money is when an asset you own falls apart. That's like your barn burning down: Something bad really has happened to you. It's holding on to a stock in the face of deterioration in the company that can cost you a packet. I am told that if you place a frog in a pan of cool water and warm it ever so slowly over the stove, Mr. Frog never makes up its mind to jump out of the pan, and so gets boiled. If, on the contrary, you drop a frog into a pan of boiling water, it of course leaps out instantly. Usually a company, or an investment theme, decays little by little. You have ample time to get out, *if you just start*. Don't let yourself get slowly boiled!

A shareholder has one big thing working for him, the underlying buildup in value—through retained earnings—of a company he owns. But many things work against him: adverse changes in the company, such as slack management or aging products; or in the industry, such as intensified competition or technological obsolescence; or in the country, in the form of heavier regulation and taxes, rising inflation, or political instability. *Do* worry about those hazards, if they are authentic and not yet reflected in the stock price. You may be sliding into a lower multiple of sagging earnings as the "glamour" aura wears off: the double play in reverse.

An extreme form is what I call the *sol y sombra* effect. In a bull ring, some seats are in the shade all afternoon, some in the sun, and some pass from sun into shade as the afternoon wears on. Similarly in a bull market, little-known stocks and new countries boom as they become "investable," but as late afternoon advances, they pass into shadow and the bids dry up completely. It's like musical chairs. So *don't get stuck with doubtful speculations going into a bear market.*

Another good reason to sell is because the reasons why you bought are no longer valid: A value stock has risen to the point where it has ceased to be good value, or a growth company's growth starts slowing.

When Not to Sell

Nevertheless, beware *rumors* of slowing growth or other troubles. They are always around, and if wrong, they become very expensive to follow. *Wait for the worry to start actually happening:* events, or management action, may forestall its occurrence.

There are two more times *not* to sell. First, solely because a great growth stock has risen splendidly. The big question is never what has the stock done, but how the *company* is doing. If it's booming along and gives every promise of continuing to do so, and *if the stock is still attractive* on an earnings basis, then certainly don't sell, unless it has become so big a part of your capital that it keeps you awake.

The second bad reason to sell is the opposite: solely because a stock has gone down. Some pundits advise selling if a stock declines 10 percent from your cost. Ridiculous! Either you understand the company or you don't. If you don't, you shouldn't own it. If you do, and if the decline is a typical market jiggle, then the logical maneuver is, if anything, to buy a bit *more.* If you're going to sell every time the stock goes down, you will never win, any more than a general who always retreats when the enemy advances. Assuming the fundamentals haven't changed, the decline may have turned your stock into a screaming buy.

Indeed, to sell a stock you understand just because it has gone down is an act of utter irrationality. It's as though after careful consideration you bought one of my perfect Labrador pups for $500, and at the same time let it be known that if anybody wanted her for $300, you'd part with her again at that price.

Fear

Professionals say that *the market climbs a wall of fear.* Quite true! If there's no fear in a stock, or a market, a decline may be imminent. What you have to establish is whether there's enough *basis* for the fear. If there isn't, the rocket is poised for a flight upward. The easiest case is the bottom of a recession, when the government is cutting interest rates, the inventory pipeline is all but empty, plant capacity utilization is down, and everybody feels awful. From that level, the next move is almost certainly up. At least it has been every few years for the last half century.

And specifically, *never sell on a war scare.* After its initial shock, the market always recovers. War is inflationary, and thus bearish for money. Things, including things represented by stocks, rise against cash in wartime.

High Capital-Gains Tax Liabilities

Older investors often feel—or are told—that they are locked in by high potential capital-gains tax liabilities. So new technologies came along, new countries, new specialties, and Grandma's ancient steels, utilities, and rail stocks remain mired in the Slough of Despond. What to do? It's like the serve in tennis: How hard you should hit is a function of how successful you are. A good investor should work off the dead position by degrees, hoping to pay the tax within a year or two by moving into something dynamic. You are better off switching during a market drop, when your stock—and its tax—are lower, along with the proposed purchase.

Trust officers may not be too unhappy with a portfolio supposedly congealed by high tax liabilities, since it gives an excuse for doing nothing while collecting the same fees. And of course immobilism is a *much* better policy than unsuccessful chipping and chopping.

Here are two useful tips:

First, you can spread the tax out into a later tax year by selling "against the box" (see "Investment Terms," at the end of the book).

Second, always give a highly appreciated stock, not cash, to charities and members of the younger generation in lower brackets than yourself.

The Tao Theory:
Mastering Your Temperament

I suspect that temperament costs investors more than ignorance. Our wonderful brain was not designed at one time, like a computer. Rather, it is a jerry-built product of long evolution, in response to changing conditions over past ages. One of its shortcomings is that we don't perceive odds correctly.* Another is that we are intoxicated by attractive ideas.† And we have had to become a social animal, meaning accepting group convictions. All these characteristics affect most of our decisions. However, we must shed them to succeed in the investment world. There we must coldly contemplate facts on the one hand and crowd emotion on the other.

The Herd Instinct

The Dow Jones Industrial Average is the encephalogram of the human race. That wiggly line reflects the limited information available to us filtered through our dreams—our hopes and our fears. Investors are profoundly affected by it—that is, by each other. While it makes no sense to get stampeded into buying or selling precipitately along with everybody else, most investors do exactly that. The herd instinct is so strong that only a handful of hardened, and perhaps slightly inhuman, souls can resist it.

---

* Some anthropologists have theorized that we take more risks than makes sense because life was once so short that we had little to lose.

† "Tell them what they want to believe," said Admiral Canaris, the German intelligence chief, speaking of effective deceptions.

There is a story of a visitor to a western town who is having his hair cut in the local barbershop, run by an incurable practical joker. After a while a crowd of people starts streaming down the street, heading out of town toward a nearby hill. When the visitor in the chair asks what is happening, the barber chuckles and says that he himself as a little joke had started a rumor earlier in the day that there would be a flood. The visitor is amused. As the town empties, however, the barber gets more and more nervous, and finally takes off his apron, puts down his scissors, and says, "I think I'd better get going myself. Don't bother to pay." The customer is astonished. But the barber, heading out the door, says, "It may be true!"

When a really good irrational panic sets in (or indeed the opposite, a bull market blowoff), very few people indeed can resist the trend. If they try to, they feel acutely uneasy. The herd instinct seems to be the strongest human emotion, one that the race is constantly breeding for as the mavericks are liquidated. Happiness is running with the crowd.

In the very nature of markets, at the bottom of a drop almost everybody you encounter will be in despair, particularly the stockbrokers, whose livelihood is caving in. Also other investors, who once felt rich and now feel poor. (In a decline, people measure down from the top. Thus, if over a year or two a stock rises from 20 to 60, then drops back to 40, its owners are depressed that it's down from 60, even though only a handful of shares may have traded at that level, rather than pleased that it has doubled from their original purchase price, which they now take for granted.)

The same herd instinct applies to companies. Your best winning idea will be a correct and original assessment of some important change in the fortunes of an enterprise you follow. The more nearly you are alone in having this idea, the safer a buy it is. So if you talk to your friends and they pooh-pooh it, you should be encouraged. But it doesn't work that way! Quite the contrary: Influenced by your friends' opinions, yearning to huddle with the herd, you lay aside your inspiration.

The way to master your temperament is to make mistakes, and then to analyze them.* Most people can't do that. Their temperament doesn't change, *so they go on repeating the same patterns*, in this as in all matters. And the extraordinary thing is that they have more confidence, not less, as they repeat the same mistakes, because they think they've learned from their previous misfortunes.

---

* *Pathe mathos*, said the Greeks: "Learn through suffering."

I've often seen intelligent investors buy too fast because they were intrigued by new ideas. And I've seen them sell completely out of great stocks on bear stories, and never buy them back, even though the stories turned out to be false and they understood the companies perfectly. ("There's no one as bearish as a sold-out bull," says Wall Street.) And then they do it again and again and again.

Some investors subconsciously want to lose money, like the inane hordes at Las Vegas or Atlantic City. The market, like the casino management, gladly accommodates them.

A silly temperamental deformation of rational investment policy occurs when one feels wedded to a stock that's dropped below cost. "I can't sell it now," you hear people say, "I have to wait until it gets back up to what I bought it for." Why? That may never happen. Women sometimes think of a disappointing stock like an unfaithful lover: After slinking from view for a time it slithers back. Then, *whack!* "Take that, you rat!" says she, swatting it with her handbag, so to speak. That is, she sells out, although thanks to good news it may be a better buy than it was originally.

Many outstanding investors find that it pays to maintain a notebook with a page for every stock you hold. Write down honestly your reasons for buying, and then later your reasons for selling. From time to time go back over your completed transactions and face up squarely to the temperamental reasons behind your mistakes, if you can.

Another investment technique is short selling. This activity is often carried on by specialized limited partnerships. You never *need* to sell short, since markets move—slowly up and rapidly down—so *cash gains against stocks in a bear market much faster than stocks gain against cash in a bull market.* Thus, raising reserves is a sufficient response to exaggerated prices. On the other hand, short selling limited partnerships try to target the most exaggerated prices. Oddly enough, though, the most crazily overpriced hyped-up junk is often what keeps rising longest in the frothy phase of a bull market. Another good category of short candidates is the most popular blue chips: They're probably overpriced. Almost all individuals, and most hedgers, find that it's safest to have a very large spread of short positions, for fear that a runaway surprise on the upside will wreck the program. One or two advisory services, including the *Zweig Performance Ratings Report* (P.O. Box 2900, Wantagh, NY 11793), have been useful in suggesting short side candidates.

The Tao of Markets

One constant of portfolio investing is cycles: Thanks to the vagaries of human nature, you can be certain that from time to time the market will become grossly overvalued or grossly undervalued. Don't *join* these cycles, *yield* to them. Benjamin Graham was fond of a little parable for this idea, which he called "Mr. Market." Think of yourself, said Graham, as owning your stocks in a joint venture with a virtual lunatic— the tens of millions of market participants transformed into a single eccentric. Every day your manic-depressive partner gets out of bed, and depending on how he feels, he offers either to buy out your share of the venture or sell you his. The offers are emotional and ill considered. For instance, one day he'll say, "Oh, God, what a mess! Look, take the whole thing at half price." And if he feels optimistic he'll say, "I feel great! How about letting me buy you out at twice market?" You need never accept any of his propositions. And except for his offers, your interest in the joint venture—the stream of profits you receive—is completely unaffected by these fits of enthusiasm or gloom. But if you want to take advantage of them, you always have that possibility. So he's a very convenient partner to have around.

In a similar vein, J. Paul Getty once made a sardonic observation to a friend of mine: "I believe in the Golden Rule," he said. "If one day I find that people are desperate to dump Getty Oil stock at less than I know it's worth, then I buy a few hundred thousand shares. And if a few years later I find they are keen to buy at almost any price, then I sell them the shares again."

Getty is really making Graham's point somewhat differently. *If you understand what you own,* you need never be preoccupied by what price the market places on it at any particular moment. As the earnings and dividends rise, the prices will in due course follow. But you can always take advantage of fluctuations to improve your average cost.

Anyway, a seasoned investor—by which I mean one who has lived through, let's say, at least three complete cycles of about four years each—can often feel in his bones where he is in the sequence. Is not the message clear when we learn that one new technology company after another zooms in price right after going public for the first time? The owners of a business don't sell their stock for love, or to enable the public to share in the benefits of the free enterprise system: They do it to make money. If they and their underwriters think that a full price for a business that they know intimately is 10, and the public jumps in and runs it up at once to 20, can we not be fairly confident that Mr.

Market has gotten out on the right side of his bed and is in a buying mood that we would be wise to take some advantage of?

A simple indicator of popular sentiment is whether closed-end funds are selling at a premium or a discount. When they are at a steep discount, it is likely that the whole market is on the cheap side and may be due for a rise. But if they are at a premium, watch out.

When the speculative pot is bubbling, then one should start getting increasingly cautious and skeptical about what's going on. But that's not what happens! I vividly remember talking to a close friend of mine who used a good, steady investment counsel firm that year in, year out beat the market, usually both in rising markets and in falling ones. He suddenly announced to me that his sister had an account that had risen 40 percent in one year with a gunslinger brokerage house, whereas his own portfolio at his steady firm had only advanced 25 percent. "I'm going to switch over to Whizkind & Co.," he said. "I don't want to miss out on the action. It doesn't happen that often. This may be my big chance."

"You're crazy," I said to him. "Have you actually looked at what they've got your sister invested in? A lot of it could be junk stocks for which there may not even be a market when this fever passes. Before you get persuaded by hot performance you've got to see how the performance is achieved, just as in mountain climbing." Well, my friend made the switch, and lived to regret it bitterly.

I'm fond of climbing, and know well that there are exceedingly few bold climbers who are also old climbers. Sooner or later the avalanche or sudden storm overtakes you by surprise, and if you're where you don't belong, you're lost. When a bull market blowoff suddenly heads south, catching you heavy in startups and concept stocks, your portfolio will be hit severely as both market and business cave in.

So relax, try to maintain an accurate concept of the value of your holdings, and if Mr. Market is in a lather to buy them, then observe the Golden Rule and throw him a bone. That's what I call the Tao of investing; giving way intelligently, just as in judo.

PART 2

The Nature of Markets

The Market Cycle and Its Choruses

J.P. Morgan was once asked what the market was going to do. He replied in his usual portentous style, "It will fluctuate." Although this seems like a putoff, it is in fact one of the most important possible truths. You need to get deeply into your bones the sense that *any market, and certainly the stock market, moves in cycles, so that you will infallibly get wonderful bargains every few years, and have a chance to sell again at ridiculously high prices a few years later.* If you grasp just that one principle, you have learned something that will let you prosper if you don't become too paralyzed to act. To avoid such paralysis, remember the "Groping for the stones" and "Boiling a frog" principles, and for this technique in action, see "The Man Who Never Lost" in the Appendixes, p. 167.

The stock market is a voting machine, polling investors on the future, not the present. Differently put, *it is a barometer, not a thermometer.* It looks ahead. In a ship, the worse the storm and the sicker the passengers, the sooner things will improve and the barometer start rising. Thus, the greatest rise in stock market history, when the Dow Jones Average doubled in less than three months, was in the summer of 1932, in the midst of a financial hurricane. Similarly, once the weather is perfect it can't get better, so the next change in the barometer will probably be down.

The first sense you have to acquire, then, is that *the worse you feel, usually because the news is bad, the safer the market is; and the better you feel, usually because the news is good, the closer you are to a top.*

Thus, by the time a new idea hits newspaper front pages or magazine covers it's usually too late to act on it. Professionals talk about the *"Business Week* cover effect"*: that excellent publication's main story on a recovery in pharmaceuticals or whatever often coincides with a market top. *Also, since all the way up in a bull market prices are higher than they were just before, stocks always seem expensive, so you are tempted to hold off buying. And since all the way down in the ensuing bear market prices are cheaper than they were before, you are tempted to plunge in too soon.*

Investment Information

A peculiarity of investment news is that *it often follows rather than anticipates price changes.* Thus, in a bull market the analysts keep revising their earnings estimates to justify the higher prices then prevailing. Pretty soon they are discounting the hereafter. And toward the bottom of a bear market you hear terrifying prophesies about disastrous possibilities that only occur every fifty or a hundred years. You are expected to believe that nobody will buy newspapers any more, that children will no longer be born, that people will no longer eat; in other words, that economic activity will all but stop. Don't believe it!

And the information will be taken in different ways, depending on the market stage. It is like a love affair: In the full tide of romantic enthusiasm all doubts are swept aside; and at the end, anything may precipitate a quarrel. In the same way, a potential weakness in a company won't hold back its stock in bull market euphoria, but will be used to justify selling when the tide turns.

These psychological cycles are easy enough to understand. The ebb and flow of mass emotion is quite regular: Panic is followed by relief, and relief by optimism; then comes enthusiasm, then euphoria and rapture; then the bubble bursts, and public feeling slides off again into concern, desperation, and finally a new panic.

The things everybody says at these times—what I call the "choruses"—are not objective data. *They are rationalizations for what is happening.* The data, particularly economic expectations, are adjusted to explain the underlying movement. Terrified customers call their brokers to seek consolation, like a bereaved widow talking to a parish priest. The answer they get is just what sounds good, the ultimate truth being opaque. I find that often the real cause of a market movement can only be discerned clearly quite a long time later.*

The market's typical emotional cycle is roughly four years from peak to peak or valley to valley, although there are plenty of exceptions. A good way to measure it is not just by stock prices, since higher company earnings may hold the market up even though the emotional cycle is fading; rather, one should probably measure it by the rise and fall of price-earnings ratios. If one plots them quarter by quarter, one sees them rising steeply, flattening, rolling over, and then falling sharply. The same company may sell at thirty times earnings at a market top, and a year later at ten times.

The usual four-year market cycle seems to be linked to the presidential elections. Typically, a defending president injects adrenaline into the economy to encourage the voters, troubled by campaign attacks and counterattacks. The election settles a number of issues, and the market, which hates uncertainty, feels relieved. The new president, now that he has to govern all the people, starts building bridges to the opposing party, rather as if Harvard and Yale had merged and one coach was running both football teams. He works to conciliate his former opponents, and for a time concord reigns. This period is often the top of the market for the four-year-cycle. Then the president starts to execute his program, and the price begins to be calculated. He also starts to detoxicate the economy from its preelection excesses, and to make painful decisions that he wants forgotten by the *next* election. All this causes withdrawal pangs, including tighter credit. Interest rates rise. The market, which is hypersensitive to higher interest rates, falls. All this is typical but there are plenty of variations and exceptions.

Similarly, there is a cycle of relatively higher and lower price-earnings ratios for the growth stocks versus the standard industrials, and for high-tech stocks within the growth sector.

Let us go through a complete cycle in a few minutes' reading, like a Disney movie that in a short time shows the growth, blossoming, and fading of a flower.

---

* William James, explaining Descartes' concept of "synoptic insight," compares current experience to climbing a mountain in a fog. You apprehend the details, but not the overall picture. Then the next day the fog lifts, and from a neighboring peak you see it all clearly. Similarly, each market phase is most easily preceived somewhat *after* the event.

The Washout: "All Is Lost!"

A convenient place to begin our circular tour is bobbing around in the pool at the base of the waterfall: In the depths of despair in a bear market—1957, 1962, 1966, 1970, 1974, 1978, 1982, or 1987. Stocks have just declined 35 percent, say, sliding several percentage points a week for months on end. Near the end of the slide many famous issues have been cut in half with terrifying speed.

At a major bottom, current business news is usually terrible, and many authorities feel that things are likely to get even worse. There are several spectacular bankruptcies, of international importance. Unemployment is usually up. There is usually some grave unresolved national problem that is bothering everybody.

The brokerage business itself is likely to be in the dumps, with many bankruptcies. Big "producers" of the up years have to cut back on their lifestyles. Wall Street's own desperation reinforces the syndrome.

When in a market collapse everything finally caves in during a few catastrophic days and weeks, there is an almost audible flushing effect. Stocks are hurled into the abyss, like the cargo of a sinking ship that the crew is desperately trying to save. Value means nothing.

About this time, if you go to a cocktail party, you will meet that irritating figure Faunty Smugg, who smoothly assures you that he hasn't owned a share for six months. A social broker you sometimes encounter, Pete Pusher, claims that he has gone short in all his accounts.

Eventually, though, a point is reached where everybody who can be scared into selling has sold. The professionals, who have been hovering overhead, so to speak, and the institutions, who always have a few billion dollars to spend, accelerate their buying, and finally an equi-

PROBLEMS

Event	Date	% Recovery from Bottom After One Year
Sputnik	October 1957	36
Steel price rollback	April 1962	30
Liquidity crunch, Penn Central bankruptcy, Wall Street failures	May 1970	40
Nixon resignation	August 1974	27
Hunt silver crisis	March 1980	29

librium is reached between the buyers and the sellers. Usually, the final battle occurs in a few days of extremely high volume—a selling climax. At this point the ordinary investor, who has gone over the waterfall, is groggy, bruised, and sick, his ears ringing. He does not want to hear about stocks, never again. The few professionals and institutions have the field pretty much to themselves. What they buy goes up, since there are almost no sellers left.

Then, some weeks later, the old lows are quietly tested on modest volume, but it doesn't attract much attention. Experienced investors are confident that better weather lies ahead. It's odd, but major bottoms are almost never a spike. They have two roots, like a tooth.

The Early Surge: "It's Too Early to Buy . . ."

So here we are at the beginning of the dynamic phase of the bull market. The optimum buying "window" will last for only a few months, but it is prudent to hold off most of your buying until the market has clearly turned, and is full and by on the new course. You can usually recognize when the upward trend has been solidly established. The professional investor does not mind paying 20 percent more for a stock that has been cut by two-thirds, to be quite certain that it is not going to go down a lot more.

The government—shocked by the decline, and as always beset by the clamor to "do something"—pumps liquidity into the economy, which of course does not take effect instantly. The Wall Street pundits declare that this time the stimulus isn't working. "It's like pushing on a rope," you hear. In fact, however, the government will get what it wants, and as soon as its intentions are fully clear, it's time to act.

The months go by and prices rise. The misery of the recent past is quickly forgotten, like a thorn extracted from your foot. A few mutual funds will have been started during the bottom area, and articles in the financial press begin pointing out that the Hercules Fund has grown 75 percent in six months. One starts hearing extraordinary stories of people who bought calls on Intertronics warrants and thus transformed $100,000 into $800,000. The institutional issues, such as the Dow stocks, make important moves. Volume, however, usually continues low. The consensus of the advisory services remains cautious.

The banks recommend staying in short-term, fixed-income instruments "until the situation has clarified." The brokers, who have to push what they can actually sell, suggest bonds, preferreds, and the like. That, however, is what I call the "yield trap." Most of the time, if bonds are going to do well, stocks will do much better. Indeed, stocks well bought at such a time will double or triple in the next few years.

The Surge Continues: "Prices Seem High . . . It's Too Late to Buy"

More months pass, and the market can now be seen to have established a rising channel for itself, like a marble rolling from side to side along a gutter. The Dow oscillates from the top of the channel to the bottom, but continues in the same broad upward path. Pete Pusher is quoted in a Wall Street newspaper as expecting one last major down leg, which will be the time to buy. There will be few significant reactions during this phase of the new bull market.

The rising prices of the principal stocks attract more buying from the professionals and from institutions who have been waiting on the sidelines; this additional buying puts prices still higher. The higher prices, in turn, give confidence to more buyers, who enter the market, putting prices higher still. The whole system continues to feed upon itself, to rise and build like a prairie twister.

The general public, during this phase, moves from feeling that it's too early to buy to feeling that it's too late to buy.

The Second Stage of the Rocket: "Prices Are High, But Maybe It's Okay to Buy . . ."

Time passes. Perhaps a year or a year and a half after the beginning, the public, which has been apathetically watching from the sidelines, starts to become interested. There are a number of downward legs, or tests, against the bottom of the market's rising channel. Each time the test is reversed at a higher level than before. The longer the channel remains intact, the more it is considered invulnerable. But the more it is considered invulnerable, the closer it is to a bust.

Most times there is eventually a pronounced and unmistakable rise in volume, which then falls off again. Later in the cycle one can usually look back and see that this volume bulge appeared approximately two-thirds of the way up the whole eventual slope. The fervor and the tempo of the dance continue to mount. The music plays louder and louder. More and more spectators join in.

Not a Cloud in the Sky: "Buy!"

More months go by, and the public is hooked. Business news is excellent. The "standard forecast" of the economic outlook is optimistic. Jazzy funds proliferate.

Some particular market area—the major industrials in 1961, the over-the-counter speculations and hedge funds in 1966, the conglomerates in 1969, the sacred-cow growth issues in 1972, the energy group in 1980, high-tech in 1983, emerging markets in 1993—surfaces as the center of attention and the focus of a self-confirming myth as the brokers and professionals bid up these "talisman" stocks to irrational heights.

The Blowoff: "Stocks Can Only Go Up"

Hot managers become famous. Young, glib, impatient of conventional wisdom, they collect huge sums from trustful and greedy investors hoping for miracles. The volume of hot manager trading may become a significant part of the whole market. They chase new themes as a pack. It then becomes profitable to jump aboard a trend (in the early 1990s, a new emerging country) instantly, before the less hot managers get hold of it and run it up. This further undermines the quality of the buying. Brokers get younger and younger, since fresh graduates swarm into the business, chasing the flood of commissions. Speculations, illiquid securities, "collectibles," commodities, and ventures are palmed off as "investments." Securities firms specializing in issues of glamour companies, or hot hedge funds, have long waiting lists for each underwriting. A broker specializing in froth can sell any stock by letting it be known that he is in touch with a few big operators who are getting behind it.

Most new issues, even of companies without a history, or even established management, rise to an immediate premium. At cocktail parties, people talk excitedly about the latest prodigy. Faunty Smugg's wife explains they are buying a shorefront house in Newport with the profits of his last six months' trading. Peter Pusher, the social broker, jumps into the market with both feet, buying his customers low-quality volatile "story" stocks and as many new issues as he can get his hands on.*

* The Japanese, whose culture requires that they all march in step, are particularly susceptible to this chorus. "Real estate in America can only go up" eventually came to mean signing up in a department store for a buying trip to California, while simultaneously taking out a $500,000 line of credit to handle any impulse purchases, like Bugsy Siegel snapping up Lawrence Tibbett's house in Hollywood with greenbacks out of a

This is what is called a buying panic—the reverse of a selling panic. It is, however, rarely profitable to jump on board a trend that has moved more than 10 percent within three months. You are indeed safer making short-term buys after the market has dropped 10 percent in two to three months. This is one of the tiny handful of tactical rules that seems to work quite well.

Why so? Because frenzy feeds on itself. The runaway horses get the bit in their teeth and gallop faster and faster. However, the runaway horses do not sprint all the way to Kansas City. At some point most experienced market operators can feel the surge becoming exhausted, and will do some buying (or selling) against the main trend, just when the most inexperienced investors are hopping belatedly on board.

Coasting: "The Market's High, But This Time Is Different . . ."

As the months wear on, stocks hesitate; their upward pace slows, with only a few leaders making new highs. The market analyst detects this situation by the loss of "breadth." For instance, the ratio of advances to declines usually starts falling, even though the leaders are still rising. Speculative volume tapers off.

And there are also inherent restraining features in a business boom:

1. Inventories eventually reach the point of glut. In the early stages of a business pickup the entire pipeline—from the mine through the mill and metalworking plant, all the way to the warehouse and hardware store—has to be replenished, so factories go on overtime. (After the peak is passed, the whole pipeline empties out again, so factories cut back.)
2. The price of raw materials is bid up as production increases.
3. Money costs go up. (In slack times, there are few borrowers, so rates are low. In a boom, the manufacturer needs more working capital to finance inventory, and wants money for plant expansion, so interest rates rise.)
4. Labor costs soar as full employment is reached, and the unions, profiting by manpower scarcity, increase their demands and get more overtime.

---

sack. The market capitalization of Tokyo real estate eventually exceeded that of the entire United States, and families would commit to a *hundred-year* mortgage to finance an apartment. When the crash came, the banks were bankrupted.

5. Efficiency drops as older facilities are brought back into production and high profits mask operating sloppiness.

Thus, beyond a certain level, more business does *not* mean higher profits; about at this point in the stock market cycle that economic fact is remembered.

A few enthusiasts still claim that this time things are different. They rationalize that the government has mastered the business cycle, so that there need not be another downturn; or that there is an absolute shortage of stocks because of an insatiable institutional or foreign appetite for them, which will support prices at permanently higher levels; or that stocks are the only refuge from inflation.

Nonetheless, in a bull market an unlimited volume of securities can be "manufactured," enough to satisfy everyone's desire to invest, however strong. "When the ducks quack, feed 'em," said the old-timers.

The Top: "Hold"

At last the government, concerned about economic "overheating" and stock market speculation, starts "leaning against the wind." The Federal Reserve raises bank reserve requirements; the discount rate goes up a notch; margin requirements may be tightened. Here again, the government gets what it wants, and in time this process always wrestles down a runaway bull market.

The insiders, suspicious of stock price levels, step up the sale of their holdings in secondary issues.

Another few months pass, and we start to recognize the typical top formation. It often comes in January, on good economic news. A series of vicious reactions, or chops, begins, probably for the first time since the cycle started. First, over a six-week period or so the market falls rapidly, perhaps 10 percent. Then the arrival of belated "second-chance" buyers halts the decline and puts the list up to new highs.

Some time later there is a second vicious chop, which usually bottoms at a higher level than the previous one. The recovery again carries to a new high. Those who sold out at the bottom of either chop feel foolish. Those who jumped in are jubilant. Peter Pusher, the social broker, says that the Dow is going up another 30 percent, "although selectivity remains important." If you sell out at about this point, you probably won't regret it. To push the operation to its limit, however, you only abandon ship when the successive chops stop reaching higher levels and start into a downward pattern, with each peak lower than the last one, and each drop going below the one before.

The secondary stocks, those not in the leading averages, have been sluggish for months.

This is the beginning of the end—a dangerous moment.

Over the Hump: "It's Too Soon to Sell"

The public remains heavily in the market, but the professional investors are edging out. They have known for some time that the most conspicuous issues are too high, and are waiting to sell as soon as they conclude that the game really is over and there is nowhere to go but down.

It is like the ogre's dinner party, at which the last guests to leave are eaten themselves. When chairs begin to be pushed back and napkins placed on the table, the wise diner prepares to dash for the exit as soon as there's any excuse to do it. *This crush at the door is why the market goes down much faster than it goes up.* The lower-quality stocks start declining significantly.

The Slide: "Prices Are Cheap, But It's Too Late to Sell . . ."

A few more months pass, and a number of issues, although not yet the leaders, have fallen appreciably from their highs, perhaps 25 percent. The mass of the market, as measured by a 2000-stock index, or, for instance, as indicated by the advance-decline ratio, has been going down for some time. Business news is now felt to be not too good. You hear doubts about the economic outlook: Perhaps there will be a recession next year?

The market, like a tired horse that no longer feels the whip, drops on bad news but fails to respond to good news, often governmental stimulation measures and bullish announcements. Still, the major brokers remain bullish on America. (They have to be, since, like companies in other industries, they have expanded their facilities, and thus lifted their break-even point, in the preceding boom.)

Faunty Smugg quietly sells his Newport establishment. He lets it be known that he has taken a few losses, but that things have come down so far "there's no point in giving up now."

"It's Okay to Sell"

After a while we may see a severe decline, with perhaps 25 percent marked off the prices of the more volatile issues. There is often a deceptive recovery, which one might call the "trap rally." It often comes in March and can last a number of weeks, producing a significant bounceback in the battered leaders. Some public investors, who were on the sidelines all the way up, are finally lured in by the lower prices. The usual sequence is that the lowest-quality stocks collapse first, while the top-quality issues struggle forward; then the general market starts giving ground. Finally, the institutional growth stocks let go, and everything starts slipping faster and faster. New and secondary public issues dry up, and indeed many old issues are so far down that the companies solicit tenders for their own shares, sometimes amounting to hundreds of millions of dollars in a month.

The Cascade: "Sell!"

Now the river sweeps over the brink, carrying everything with it. A cardinal point of market strategy, if you are a trader at all, is to get out before this cascade, even if one has already lost 15 or 20 percent.

Business news is bad. The standard forecast is for more stormy weather ahead. The hot fund managers have to meet redemptions, but find out that illiquid securities can't be sold and depart in disgrace. As for the margin operators and leveraged funds, their borrowings turn out only to have hurried them to disaster. (Aggressive managers as a class lose more money than they make, because you can only raise money for aggressive vehicles when the pot is bubbling, and the lessons of the previous collapse have been forgotten. This kind of money comes in most readily when the cycle is nearer its end than its beginning. Relatively little money is thus in the aggressive pools of capital on the way up, and a lot more on the way down.)

The Selling Climax: "The Market's Going Way Down . . ."

The torrent crashes down the falls. In the frightful plunge some stocks give up in a day their gains of a year, and drop 30 percent in a week. Pete Pusher urges his customers to sell before they lose everything. It is so sudden and so awful that for a while many investors can't quite believe it. When the smallest investors finally throw in the sponge and sell out, it turns up in the newspaper figures as odd-lot short sales. The man who can't afford to deal in hundred-share lots goes to his broker so sure that the end is at hand that he sells short seventeen shares, say, of GE, hoping to buy them back for a lot less after the cataclysm. This paroxysm of odd-lot despair often takes place right at the bottom of the market, during what is called the selling climax. Such a climax does not always occur, but when it does, an experienced investor can feel it clearly. Fairly often it comes in October. For years I've wondered why. One possibility is that October is when the crops move from the field into the barn, and a risky crop loss becomes a solid one on inventory.

So here we are again, four years or so after we started out, half drowned, bones broken, washed out, all passion spent.

But if you've kept some reserves intact, and have the knowledge to recognize real value when it's being dumped by panicky, uninformed sellers, and have the guts to act, then at these moments you can make the buys of a lifetime. We've had eight economic storms since World War II. During almost all of them investors became convinced that the skies would never clear and the sun shine again. But it always does.

Crises

I have mentioned that one should try to determine the main trend of the market, and then look for buying opportunities during reactions against that trend.

An infallible formula for this exercise is buying during crises, particularly war scares. Wars are inflationary, thus they are bearish for money compared to things, including things represented by stocks in companies. The immediate shock of a war scare, death of a president, or other crisis creates an imbalance in the market that forces prices too far down.

One solution is to buy six-month or one-year calls, if they are reasonably priced. Your broker will have to help you determine that.

The Wall Street Waltz

Think of the market as a dance. First one and then another participant joins in the fun, and in due course, exhausted, drops out again. The dancers are always the same ones, but they are not always active; some are usually on the sidelines. There are five or so of them: the public, institutions, companies and company insiders, the professionals—including computer-generated trading programs—and foreign investors. The government also intervenes at rare intervals, but decisively. And the finale is almost always that time's version of the speculative orgy on full margin.

1. The Public

The 40-odd million individual public investors are usually gradually buying or selling year after year, these days mostly through mutual funds. But when they are gripped strongly by mass emotion—euphoria or panic—for a while they can hurl the market about like a hurricane shaking a forest. Through the 1970s and 1980s, individual investors were sellers of stocks, first to pension funds and then in the 1980s to corporate buyers who were taking advantage of market prices below what private buyers would pay for the same assets. Now corporations are selling again, and the public has come swarming back in. Recently it has been responsible for more than three-quarters of all such stock purchases. Stocks have risen from 19 percent of family financial assets in 1974 to 25 percent by early 1994, reversing the decline from 39 percent of family assets to 19 percent after the horrible 1974 crash, when the disillusionment of the public put a cap on the market for eight years.

Professionals carefully follow the cash position of mutual funds. One might think that the big funds, with their superior wisdom, would be buying at bottoms and selling at tops. Alas, it's just the opposite: They are most heavily in cash near major bottoms, so they can cope with redemptions, and have least cash at major tops. In a bull market, the intense buying is in speculative funds. On the way down they experience substantial redemptions, but it is not easy to sell speculative stocks. So these funds are likely to fall even faster than they rose.

One reason the public acts so violently is its ignorance, which means that both panic and euphoria grip it more violently than, say, the professionals, just as a mob of green militia is easily scattered by a few battle-hardened veterans. To give an example, a survey conducted by the SEC in 1993 found that 49 percent of investors thought that the government insured funds bought through banks. If they suddenly discover that the government backing they have counted on isn't there, these buyers may panic.

2. Institutions

Institutional investors—notably pension funds, insurance companies, bank trust departments, and mutual funds—have been steadily growing in importance, and often provide most of the trading volume in the stock market. The first two always have new money coming in, and thus are in a position to invest at bottoms (at least a little) when others are petrified with fear.

In quiet periods, institutions move slowly and majestically, and regard capital preservation as their cardinal duty. When from time to time some of them are caught up in the rapture of the dance, they hire go-go operators to whirl their portfolios around in the "stories" that are throbbing just then. But only a few of the "story" stocks survive the sharp ax of the next bear market. So the institutions, chastened, fire their go-go managers, and go back to trying to preserve capital.

3. Companies and Company Insiders

Remember that while there are lots of reasons for an insider to sell, including exercising stock options, getting his estate liquid, or buying a house or financing a divorce, there is only one reason to buy:

To make money. *So pay attention to company and company insider buying.*

A company repurchasing its own shares is showing great confidence in the stock value. And even company insiders can sometimes move the market price of a small or medium-sized enterprise to where it belongs. A company with a market capitalization of $50 million or so may have an insider group, including the founders and their families, that owns 40 percent of the shares—$20 million. There is nothing to stop these insiders from buying or selling as they please, although in due course they have to file a report with the SEC. Suppose the company is experiencing good times. As cheerful tidings are announced, the stock goes up. But the insiders, including not only the executives but the directors and their friends, and customers of brokers close to the situation, will often have been buying for some time. In such cases, an outside investor should assume that the insiders have moved the stock close to its reasonable price. It would be bold of him to suppose he knows something they don't. That's why an old Wall Street maxim suggests that you *"buy on the rumor and sell on the news."* Insider trading is monitored by a number of subscription services, e.g., Consensus of Insiders, P.O. Box 10247, Fort Lauderdale, FL 33334-0001.

4. The Professionals

Professional investors include floor traders, hedge funds (some of which now rank as institutions), major investors, principals of Wall Street firms trading for their own account, and the like. They control hundreds of billions of dollars. I am sorry to say that some of them occasionally get together with their allies and "run" a stock, just like the pool operators in the bad old days before the SEC. So, if you buy a much-touted, thinly traded issue, ask someone knowledgeable on Wall Street matters about its sponsorship.

Computer-generated program trading is an interesting subcategory that becomes important at particular moments, namely, when the machines decide all at once to lurch this way or that. I think that the net effect of such episodes has so far been just to increase market volatility, and thus to create opportunities for those who know at what price they want to buy or sell. I doubt if program trading has an effect on the long-term direction of the market.

5. Foreign Investors

Foreign investors form the last category, which used to be a minor factor in Wall Street trading and was found on the wrong side of the market, buying at stops and selling at bottoms. The Italian department store executive sees his holdings dropping day by day and week by week. Cut off from knowing what is really happening, he decides that matters must be terribly sick. IBM is going out of business, the stock will hit zero. So will everything else. In desperation he calls up his banker in Lugano to instruct him, in guarded language, to switch the family's stock portfolio into Treasury bills or gold. This usually happens right at the bottom, as part of the selling climax. Being far from the scene of action robs one of a sense of reality and intensifies both panic and euphoria.

The Japanese suffer from the weakness of their strength, a willingness to act in concert. That works well in corporate life and in war, but is disastrous in investing. Most recently the Japanese paid top dollar for enormous amounts of U.S. inner-city commercial real estate.

6. The Government—"Don't Fight City Hall"

When the government is determined to put the brakes on a runaway boom, it has the instruments. An excellent old Wall Street rule goes, "Three steps and stumble." When the government is raising interest rates or margin requirements or bank reserve requirements at the Fed, it does not do so with a single drastic movement like a slash with a saber. Rather, like a boa constrictor strangling a pig, it gradually increases the pressure until the victim suffocates. This may involve five or ten little stages. But eventually, as I say, the government gets what it wants. Therefore, if you see three consecutive moves in the same direction, such as three discount rate increases, you can reasonably assume that the Fed is signaling its wishes, and that prudence dictates that you get out of the way.

A standard Wall Street joke has it that the market discounted five of the last three recessions. The reason is simply that the market resembles the lookout on a ship's crow's nest. When he starts screaming about rocks, the people on deck take notice. A severe market decline often shocks the government into taking strong countermeasures. Society has a powerful instinct for self-preservation, and will ordinarily force a government to respond to powerful signals. But when? Usually, so late that the problem has already self-corrected, and the government's measures overstimulate the recovery that is already in progress.

7. Theme and Variation: The Disguised Margin Account

Most great bull market tops are that time's excuse for a margin account. As stocks go up, week after week, month after month, and year after year, investors say to themselves, "Since I'm such a devilish clever fellow and doing so brilliantly, why don't I borrow a bit to buy twice as much, so that I can make even more?"

But for the process to function, each occasion requires a different presentation. It's like a seedy nightclub: The jaded customer watches the different acts going by, and may or may not realize that they are all the same girls, in different costumes. One time they are cowgirls with leather boots and revolvers, next time a tango team. Always the same old troupe in slightly altered form. In just this way the market serves up a series of disguised margin accounts as part of every great top.

Back in the 1920s, individuals ordinarily speculated on full margin. That is, they borrowed from their brokers up to 90 percent or so of the value of the stocks they held. That meant that they could be wiped out overnight, and since everything happens sooner or later, when the Great Crash came, they were.

The same principle also took the form of the leveraged trusts, of which Tri-Continental is the principal survivor. Investment companies were floated composed not only of common stock but also preferred stocks, debentures, and bonds; the whole bundle was then invested in stocks. Thus, if the market rose 10 percent, the shares of the leveraged trust might go up 20 percent or 30 percent. The volatility of the trust's own stock was prodigious . . . in both directions. In time, of course, the leveraged trusts collapsed, so this exact form of the margin heresy became embedded in Wall Street memory.

In the 1960s, companies used to acquire other companies in unrelated industries with packages of securities called "Chinese paper." This, of course, weakens the balance sheet of the acquiring company, although if things go well, it will prosper. Since the companies bought were in different industrial areas, the earnings of the group would be more stable, it was asserted. Their incongruities would stimulate management through "synergism." When the acquisitor company sold at a higher price-earnings ratio in the market than the companies it bought, this game gave it better and better reported earnings and higher book values after each transaction, which made it more and more careless about what it acquired. One of the most famous instances was ITT under Harold Geneen, which clocked off year after year of higher reported earnings using this technique, until its companies—and the debt incurred to acquire them—became unmanageable. The archetypal example was the Ivar Krueger debacle in Swedish Match: eventually his accumulation of companies became an overleveraged jungle. It collapsed, and the Match King committed suicide.

A recurring variation is the hedge fund. Their leverage is supposed to be all right because the manager owns the stocks he likes and sells short the ones he doesn't, so everything is balanced and thus purportedly safe. The problem is that in the frothy phase of a runaway bull market the hottest managers can take in hundreds of millions of dollars a month, so many do not in fact hedge, which would dampen their performance. They run a margin account, pure and simple, except that the limited partners don't catch on until it's too late.

The leveraged buyout mania using junk bonds has been a vast disguised margin account. That time the rationale was that if management had a bigger share of ownership, it would work harder to produce better earnings to pay down the debt incurred to finance the purchase. Often management does indeed work harder, but trying to stave off bankruptcy.

Investors of the future will look back at our period and marvel that we did not recognize the multiplication of derivative instruments as our time's variation of margin account. (They will of course fail to perceive their own time's variation.) The volume of transactions in commodity and currency derivatives vastly exceeds the transactions in the actual goods involved. Futures and other such confections offer investors a bigger bang for the buck, while everything is going up. Mutual funds consisting entirely of warrants have been floated, and some of the very largest hedge funds engage primarily in currency speculation. It's not that different from the South Sea Bubble days. But bubbles pricked by the unforeseen needle always burst.

Winning Strategies:
Change As the Times Change

In the course of studying investment history, and as a practitioner myself, I have found that you can do extraordinarily well by noticing a neglected great market inefficiency and taking advantage of it early. In fact, that is the essence of many great investment successes. Here are some examples:

1. *Underpriced Common Stocks.* In the 1920s, Edgar Lawrence Smith proposed common stocks as a proper trust investment, in addition to the traditional bonds and real estate, in his seminal book, *Common Stocks as a Long-Term Investment,* published by Macmillan in 1924. A great truth! Trustees who accepted this idea in the 1930s saw the value of their assets increase astronomically.

2. *Systematic Security Analysis.* In those days, good investing meant buying physical assets—jigs and dies, bricks and mortar—at a discount from book value. In the 1930s and 1940s, Benjamin Graham elaborated on this concept by developing for the first time a systematic technique of security analysis, using only widely available financial information. His followers, of which the best known today is Warren Buffett, achieved consistent gains using his methods.

3. *Trading Blue Chips.* By the early 1950s, a few economically sophisticated firms achieved exceptional results by trading industrial blue chips, following rotating strength in successive sectors of the economy as the business cycle evolved, or as outside events intervened. For instance, higher oil prices bring splendid profits to the producers,

but can be ruinous for airlines. The firm I then worked for ran the best-performing fund of the decade using this technique.

4. *Growth Stocks.* In the latter 1950s the idea of "growth stocks," leading companies in growth industries, which increase their earnings from market cycle to market cycle, was put forward by T. Rowe Rice as an alternative to Graham's bargain-hunting approach. Examples would be 3M and American Home Products. Owning specialty growth stocks has proved to be a particularly attractive variation, and year in, year out still seems to me to be the private investor's best single strategy.

5. *Service Companies.* In the early 1960s the idea became increasingly accepted that service companies, such as investment banking firms and advertising agencies whose stock in trade is chiefly people and goodwill, could be outstanding holdings even though they owned no hard assets. Indeed, some are now considered to be among the best investments, since they are less subject to obsolescence than are manufacturing companies.

6. *Hedge Funds.* In the same period, investment manager A. W. Jones, who is often credited with the popularization of the hedge fund, developed the idea that it sharpens a superior manager's technique to have some short positions counterbalancing his long positions. This difficult game is now quite common, and some of the most extraordinary recent performances have been achieved by hedge fund operators.

7. *Foreign Stocks.* A few analysts such as John Templeton, John Clay, and Harry Seggerman recognized very early the outstanding values available in Japanese (and other) foreign equities.

8. *Smaller Companies.* In general, there are better values in good small companies than good large companies. Some managers have carried this principle abroad, so far very successfully. Smaller companies have for many years been a most attractive market area, and in general seem to outperform larger companies, particularly during recoveries from market bottoms. Inactive stocks are the profitable specialty of a handful of firms.

9. *Emerging Markets.* Most countries, including the United States and Japan, were considered "emerging" at one time. The lifting of the Communist threat has created a huge boom in Asia and South America.

10. *Business Franchises.* The first chapter in my book *The Money Masters*, which appeared in 1980, was on Warren Buffett, who went on

to become the richest man in history to make his fortune entirely through classical investing techniques. I later published a whole book on Buffett, called *The Midas Touch* (HarperCollins, 1988). Buffett's central idea has been the strength of certain business franchises, notably monopoly daily newspapers, TV státions, and entrenched brand names, such as Coca-Cola and Gillette.

11. *Rerating International Debt Issuers*. It has proved possible to make good profits by investing in the debt issues of countries that are reforming their economies, before the benefits are fully understood by the markets. One private fund specializing in this technique gained 80 percent in 1993. Some recent examples have included Ecuador and Panama.*

12. *Junk Bonds*. Michael Milken exploited a pricing error in the lower-quality bond end of the fixed-income spectrum. In financial terms, this was like discovering that $E=mc^2$: it unlocked a huge store of value. Alas, he and his discovery went too far.

13. *Mergers and Acquisitions*. During the wave of takeovers in the 1970s and 1980s, broker Mario Gabelli and many others bought shares in acquisition candidates, waiting for offers to be received at higher prices.

14. *High Technology*. Most investors and investment managers are baffled by high technology, which nevertheless can be an extremely rewarding investment area. You have to operate through a specialist, with access to scientific knowledge.

15. *"Macro" Bets*. Fortunes have been made through leveraged bets on, e.g., movements between major currencies, the direction of European interest rates, and overpricing in Japanese banks.

16. *Distressed Securities and Arbitrage*. A number of managers are consistently successful in buying neglected senior securities in corporate reorganizations, or convertible securities that are incorrectly priced in relation to their underlying common stocks, or stocks of merging companies that are incorrectly priced in relation to each other.

* Of course, they will get in trouble all over again and again be reformed. My cousin George Francis Train restructured the external debt of Panama over fifty years ago. The cycle is endless.

There are two main advantages to what I call the "diversified strategies approach" to investing: First, one can spread risk by using different strategies that do not move together. And second, one may be able, if one dares be original, to take advantage of new approaches before they become overexploited. The "groping for the stones" technique—starting on a small scale to see how things work—makes this easier.

Any successful market approach will become too popular. The rate of return then declines, or "regresses to the mean." So one has to remain alert. That means carefully monitoring outside "masters," and watching for new developments. A good sign is when a formerly successful strategy has become overexploited and then collapsed, so that it can't be sold any more. Real estate investment trusts, for instance, stagger from booms to busts. Often those managers, after a decade in which their technique didn't work, actually move right out of the field. Growth investment became discredited in 1974, when actually it was most attractive, and the growth analysts who had been pulling down huge salaries a couple of years previously became redundant. Almost all short-side partnerships have been forced out of business as I write in 1994, at a time when there are grotesque overvaluations in the IPO (initial public offering) market, which invite short selling.

Losing Strategies:
Beware Simple Answers

In investing, as in politics, the easy, plausible notion is often misleading.

1. Technical Analysis

Nothing is as enticing as a neat predictive system. Everybody wants them, which is why astrologers and fortunetellers proliferate. But the economy is unpredictable, and the nature of the Wall Street game evolves constantly. So by the time you have adjusted to a system, you can count on the rules changing. It is very easy indeed to carry out a computer playback of any given strategy. In statistics this is called "data mining," and is a well-known trap. For a few tens of thousands of dollars you can discover what could have worked until yesterday. But to analyze how the previous rules are changing . . . that's the problem! I know dozens of investment management companies that have spent millions and millions of dollars on this quest. They have almost always failed in due course.* So the average investor is much better advised to abandon the whole subject of systems and formulas.

In a market situation, the reaction to an event changes that event. When the radar warns that danger is approaching the pilot changes course. In physics, this is called "feedback." *In human affairs, the effects of feedback cannot be expressed mathematically by a formula,* at

---

* The most recent is Paul Tudor Jones, an extremely good investment manager, who in 1986 set up Tudor Systems Corp. to replicate his thinking, using computers. Late in 1993, after an outlay in seven figures, the project was abandoned.

least not yet. Judging human reactions is a matter of intuition, based on flair and experience.

The most familiar form of the Simple Answers fallacy is technical analysis. In reality, it's the opposite of technical: it resembles tea-leaf reading. To buy a house after you've looked it over carefully with an expert is what I'd call technical; to buy a stock on the basis of patterns and price action, without looking at the underlying business, is neither technical nor, indeed, analysis.

How many defunct technical systems one remembers is a function of how long one has followed Wall Street. People say that when formulas become too widely followed, they perforce become ineffective precisely because their followers jam up. Not so. No formula has become that popular. It's just that the whole market changes, and so the formulas should change too, but don't. You have to be able to analyze the change, and translate it into action. That's not simple.

God save us from the short-term reader/advisors who look for shapes—"rounding bottoms," "pennants," "head and shoulders tops," and the like—usually called *charting*. I find charting as a matter of practical experience to be useless. In fact, there seems to be some negative correlation. Why so? Because enough people believe in these things so that when it is announced that a "head-and-shoulders bottom" has occurred, the public moves in and knocks the market slightly off balance. When matters resume their normal course, the distortion is corrected—at the speculator's expense.

Another technical device that I am suspicious of is buying a stock that is going up because the chart is "strong."* By the time a stock's strength is evident, it's often so late in a move that you are approaching a change in direction.

2. Market Analysis

I think much more highly of *market analysis* than of charting. Market analysis is like putting a suspect on a lie detector to get more data than is obvious from just looking at him. That can be useful for the investigator, although the courts rightly refuse to consider it conclusive. If stocks are by traditional criteria cheap in relation to bonds, if they are selling well below replacement cost, if times are hard and investors are gloomy, then you should feel more confident. If times are booming and investors are full of confidence, than you should get ready to ease off

* Also called *momentum* or *flow of funds investing*.

for a while. A high market can go much higher, though, so market analysis can help tell you where you are, but not necessarily what comes next.

Here is a confession: I have always been fascinated by this subject. Years ago, before I was married, I spent many evenings at it. I even discovered one tool that is now used quite extensively. It occurred to me that the degree of popular frenzy in the stock market at any time could be measured by comparing the volume on the American Stock Exchange (formerly the Curb, because it was actually held out on the street), where the more speculative companies trade, with the volume on the staider New York Stock Exchange. To get the old records, I sent my assistant to the Amex. She dug them out, copied them, and brought them back. I plotted these records and found that, historically, Curb and American Stock Exchange trading had run around 10 percent of New York Stock Exchange volume. If it ever got up to over 50 percent and stayed there for a while, you knew you were in a period of wild speculation. When ASE volume then collapsed, you know you were witnessing the pricking of the speculative balloon, and that in a few months the whole market would probably come tumbling after. To my knowledge, this method has often failed to give a signal, but has never given a misleading one. In correspondence with other professionals on this phenomenon, I called it the "Tessa Index," since my assistant (the daughter of the founder of the Commandos, as it happens), bore that name. Long after, Tessa passed into the standard lingo as the "Speculation Index."

I find several other such tools interesting, including the consensus of advisory services, which is widely tracked. A strong consensus is usually wrong, since advisory services, like politicians, generally follow trends, echoing their readers' hopes and fears. Mutual fund cash is another barometer; high cash levels signal bottoms, and low cash levels signal tops. Another good one is how many stocks are selling for less than their cash in the bank. These indices may reveal that investors' actions are approaching some historical limit, from which a change of tack becomes inevitable.

However, some of the favorite market analysis indicators, like most of the charting patterns, are superstitions. For instance, there are pundits who rely on the so-called January Indicator. It prescribes that if the stock market rises in January, then it will be up for the whole year, so you should watch what January brings, and then act. Obviously, in this system the eleven months following January are what counts: You buy at the start of February and get rich. Alas, that simply doesn't work. If January is up, the year is indeed usually up, but only *including January*, when you were waiting for your sign. The eleven subsequent months don't necessarily make you money.

3. In-and-Out Trading

Only a handful of professionals are consistently successful at a strategy of in-and-out trading, which is costly in commissions and in your time. The retail investor should avoid it. *Decide whether what you propose to buy is a "bump" stock that you hope will make a specific upward move, or a "cruise" stock that you hope will go on rising for a long time.* Sign on for the cruise, rather than the bump.

4. "Blue Chip," "Glamour," and "Religion" Stocks

The object of one's investment quest is to find the desirable under-priced asset. A *glamour* stock is a growth company that is in the spotlight at a particular time; a *blue chip* is an established enterprise whose merits are fully (maybe overly) recognized by banks and other investment institutions, and is probably overpriced. None will offer a neglected opportunity. *Religion stocks* are death. In fact, the words, "U.S. Whizzo can only go up," are *a fire bell to the seasoned investor*. When you hear them, you can be sure that all are aboard the stock who are going to get aboard.

Similarly, promising industries that have been around long enough to excite investors usually make at least temporarily disappointing investments. *A sign of an overpopular industry comes when stocks or mutual funds change their names to sound as though they were part of it*—notably the periodic booms in "-onics" and "-etics" stocks. Either look ahead for what's just surfacing, before it attracts wild popular enthusiasm, or wait for a growth industry's second wind, as selectivity corrects the initial rapture.

5. New Ventures

The simplest argument against investing in new ventures, unless one is a specialist, goes like this: A new venture usually consists of a business opportunity propelled by an entrepreneurial group and some stock salespeople. But the proposed managers may or may not be up to their tasks, and the business will probably not succeed even if they are.

In any case, the entrepreneur, the proposed management, and the selling group will usually ask for about half the company in return for their development work—having the idea, putting up the initial money, organizing the deal into presentable form, and (as to the proposed management) leaving their former jobs. These propositions are hard to sell, so the selling group also earns a hefty compensation. Thus, for all the cash they put in, the investors typically get only about half the venture. Moreover, they enter an exceedingly risky situation. Perhaps one new venture in ten survives, and only a small percentage of those that survive become highly successful. Frequently they evolve into "teasers," requiring additional rounds of capital—with severe dilution for the original investors—before becoming airborne (or crashing). Remember, too, that the most interesting deals are shown first to the professional venture-capital firms, not the public.

The patient investor in listed stocks, on the contrary, can be confident that once every four years or so, shares in some of the finest companies in the world—with outstanding records, assured futures, and superb management in place—will be offered in a market washout at far less than the whole company would go for in a negotiated sale.

So why pay a dollar for fifty cents' worth of an uncertain proposition, when with less risk and study, and only a little patience, it will buy you two dollars' worth of an outstanding enterprise?

6. Exciting New Issues

Be wary of exciting new issues, particularly in a bubbling market, and *most particularly of companies that are not yet making money*. They are made to sound—and thus to sell in the market—better than they are likely to be. Think of it this way: Suppose I made a fist, promised you that I was holding a banknote in it, and asked you if you would make a firm bid on it. Your only reasonable answer is no. Imagine that the thing in my fist is a ten-dollar bill. If you bid $5, I'll refuse. If you bid $20, you've got a bad deal. Similarly, in new issues the company and its bankers know a lot more than you do, and are setting a price that's attractive to the sellers.

Dr. Porter K. Wheeler studied 3,000 equity new issues in the 1980s, which raised over $55 billion. He showed that 58 percent of them had some sort of market quotation at the end of the decade. Of those, three-quarters had done worse than the market.

7. Big Economic Ideas

One cannot as a practical matter use big economic ideas successfully in the daily business of investing. A good growth stock goes its own way, and if a knocked-down value stock is cheap enough, the economy is irrelevant. In *The New Money Masters* I quote Peter Lynch as saying that economics is a subject on which he spends "about fifteen minutes a year." Almost none of the "masters" I have studied is interested in economic predictions. If, however, there is a consensus as to the economic outlook—higher interest rates ahead, a recession impending—the long odds, and therefore the safer bet, will probably be on the other side.

One exception may be *assessing supply and demand in particular industries.* Regulation can hold down the supply of something until a shortage develops, such as natural gas under regulated pricing in the 1970s, or gold before the Nixon administration took us off the fixed price. (See number 1 of "Train's Laws.") When you observe demand building up acutely in this way, a price explosion should only be a question of time.

8. Investment Gimmicks

Investment gimmicks include commodities, option programs and, for an individual investor, games using derivative instruments, where there is no intrinsic buildup of value, just a casino. Most of these approaches are expensive in commissions and fees. An aggressive commodity-trading operation can easily devour 50 percent of one's equity in annual commissions, an impossible handicap to overcome. (See "Commodities Trading," in the Appendix "Bad Deals and Pitfalls.") To be convinced, just look at the investment records of funds practicing one of the gimmick approaches, such as selling options. Almost never are they successful over long periods. The performance records of such funds are very often misleading. *And remember that many that existed ten years ago have just vanished; only the successful survivors like to display their records.*

The essence of your investment quest is buying a share of a business at an unusually favorable price. Gimmicks probably won't work, and worse, will distract you from what does.

PART 3

Alternatives

When to Buy "Hard" Assets

Inflation tortures both stocks and bonds. Most companies have trouble passing on inflationary cost increases to the consumer. The authorities will in due course put up interest rates to combat inflation, which crushes both the stock and bond markets. During an inflationary boom, therefore, people turn from stocks and bonds to "hard" assets: real estate, art, and "collectibles."

In a noninflationary boom, companies—and thus financial assets—shine, so people turn to common stocks and their equivalents.

During a noninflationary recession, bonds are satisfactory: Poor business conditions mean that companies do not borrow, so the government opens the credit spigot, and interest rates drop. Thus interest rates fall, and prices of existing bonds rise.

Here, then, is a diagram of the indicated strategies for various conditions:

	Inflation	**Disinflation**
Boom	Art, real estate, and other "hard" assets	Stocks
Recession	Short-term debt; gold	Long-term bonds*

* Particularly when the yield curve is inverted (see Investment Terms, p. 198).

Investing in Land

Throughout history, raw land has been a "store of value" for the very long-term passive investor who wanted to preserve excess present earning power for future use.

The real problem now is local government regulation. You can have studied an acquisition with care, bought well, wangled favorable rezoning, gotten a special permit to build, lined up financing, and then, after years of effort and interest charges, lose your zoning and have to start all over again, with less hope of success. Or of course you may never get the necessary zoning in the first place.

And even if you get and keep all your zoning and special permits, you can easily fall afoul of environmental regulations—not only existing regulations but future ones. Furthermore, when an existing developer has gotten what he wants, he has an incentive to prevent the next person from following him. Once inside the fortress, he pulls up the drawbridge. He thinks of your neighboring acres as a park, which it is his ecological duty to keep green forever.

You're only secure when you've not only received the necessary zoning and your special permit to do the particular thing desired, but have also "appropriated the land to the use," to use the technical term. This means taking physical steps that advance the purpose contemplated in the special permit. That's why you so often find that immediately after he has gotten his special permit, a buyer digs a huge foundation hole or lays pipe or strings wires.*

---

* Abroad, you may not be safe even then. In Italy, permission is sometimes simply revoked, and I know of cases in Venezuela in which a rival developer bribed the clerk of the Consejo Municipal to alter the records of years earlier.

If you really do want to invest in land, here are some suggestions. The first is to buy where there's going to be development: in the path of progress. You're usually safest buying near where you live. You should have a better idea of the values, you'll be an "insider" when it comes to zoning and special permits, and you'll see with your own eyes what's going on.

To be reasonably sure of the market later on, you should buy where there is continuous interest, such as in the spillover of a growing city, or in a resort area. Water is a great attraction. One should consider also places where energy sources are being discovered. Development follows cheap energy.

If you want to buy around a city, then you need to look where growth is coming. That takes study and a friend in City Hall. *Lots of people around city government have a clear idea of what's coming.* Buying a bargain-priced tract in a declining area may mean there's no development interest when you want to sell, and so no market. The optimal strategy is to buy just ahead of possible development interest: *in the late predevelopment stage.*

A real estate advisor will prepare you a map of the target area with overlays showing existing zoning and land uses, utilities, public transportation, proposed roads, planned and rumored developments, and other factors. After a while, the logical areas for development often emerge.

Your terms of payment are important. You have to be able to hold the property comfortably for the five years or so required to get the various permits. Consider paying with five notes, payable annually, each bearing the agreed interest rate but each separate, so that at the end of the first year you only pay interest in cash on the first note, and so on. Thus, for a $1 million purchase paid with five $200,000 notes at 8 percent, you only pay $16,000 interest in cash the first year, not $80,000 as you would have to if you paid with a single note. Leverage, of course, works in both directions, like stock market margin. If you borrow or finance to buy, and development takes too long—as it often does—you may be squeezed right out.

There is an advantage to buying in an area where there's already favorable zoning and where resort amenities are available, since for many people a land investment doubles as the site of a possible retirement home. One should be near such activities as a country club with a golf course and tennis courts, or a yacht club with a marina and swimming pool, together with a clubhouse or hotel and perhaps bungalows where visitors can stay during their holidays. Like migratory birds, some will get used to coming to the area; when the time comes, they will be candidates for home purchase.

Unfortunately, there are only a handful of really good resort developers in the United States, and if the manager of yours is not outstanding, you have no assurance that it will still be attractive when you want to cash in on your lot.

Making money in land is at least as hard as making money in the stock market, and one should approach the problem with great respect. It pays any investor in land to hire a consultant. There are hundreds of things to check, many of which never occur to an inexperienced buyer. The Society of Real Estate Appraisers and the Society of Real Estate Counselors can both furnish you lists of appraisers and consultants in the area you're interested in. It's particularly foolish to rely on the broker. Remember, *by law the broker represents only the seller.* You may get on cozy terms with him (often her), but your interests are divergent.

Don't be lulled into making bad land investments by the old cliché, "They're not making any more of it." Maybe they're not, but you could put the whole United States population into Texas and it still wouldn't be as densely populated as Great Britain. There's no real shortage of space in this country.

If there is a Real Estate Investment Trust (REIT) in your area whose properties you can get a line on and whose management is completely honest, you can participate in the long-term enhancement of property values by picking up shares when they are known to be at a sharp discount from underlying values. This happens surprisingly often.

Buying Land on Trips

I once had a friend I'll call Milner, who was a water-supply consultant, mainly to cities in developing countries. Over the years he had spent a week or two in a hundred or so different cities in the Third World. There weren't many where he couldn't tell you the hotel of choice or some attractive, reasonably priced restaurants.

Milner developed an interesting routine. He would occasionally take half a day off in a city he liked and go for a drive in the suburbs with a real estate agent. He would try to figure out in what direction the city was destined to grow (often it's upwind, and usually toward the airport). Then he'd buy a little patch of raw land out there for a few thousand dollars. He practically never sold a property; he just paid the taxes, and read a report that a local lawyer would send him once a year on how things looked.

It's hard to get rich in the water-supply consulting business, but Milner has now become one of the more prosperous of my contemporaries. Ten years ago when I ran into him in Bangkok, he took me on his rounds with his local real estate agent. We looked at a piece of land he had bought out in the suburbs in the fifties. Milner's tract, on the way to the airport, was still something of a no-man's-land, although some commercial structures were beginning to sprout in the area. Recently I again passed through Bangkok, and was astonished to find a low-rise office building on the plot.

When Milner first showed me his little holding, he mentioned that he thought its value was about $25,000, compared to his cost of $2,200. I expect that by the time I saw it recently, after he'd parlayed it into an interest in an office building, it could scarcely have been worth less than $1 million.

Another place where Milner performed this stunt was Yuma, Arizona, which was for a long time one of the fastest-growing towns in one of our fastest-growing states. Here he drove out in a rented car, studied the direction in which he thought development was likely to go, and later wrote from home to a local real estate broker, asking him to find a tract to buy for a couple of thousand dollars at most. The tract is now downtown, and has increased enormously in value.*

Milner preferred to buy in troubled countries. Any market is manic-depressive, and local political problems cause real estate prices to fluctuate more than they should. In bad times the buyers melt away, and since somebody always has to sell, you have the field to yourself, as though you were the only bidder at an auction. But countries almost never disappear from the economic map. Society has a strong instinct for self-preservation. If the landowners in Athens or Buenos Aires are desperate to unload some property, why not buy a bit? And if a few years later they are hell-bent to buy it back, why not oblige them?

To be sure, Milner had had some turkeys. He lost money on plots outside Beirut and, so far, Montevideo. In all, however, on a total investment of less than $100,000 spread over about twenty years, Milner now has land assets worth tens of millions. Today the stakes re-

---

* Sam Walton of the Wal-Mart chain liked to fly his own plane over a town where he was thinking of putting a store, to sense the drift of growth. Anti-big-government magnate Ross Perot was often observed riding a horse around the immense tract between Dallas and Fort Worth that he eventually developed—to no small extent with adroitly wangled government money.

quired to play Milner's game are higher, but it still works, and adds spice to a trip. *Bon voyage!*

"The Real Estate Man's Prayer"

I cannot close this section without mentioning "the real estate man's prayer." A group of my clients had made several tens of millions of dollars by developing some buildings. In real estate, you tend to "mortgage out"—get your money back by hocking your developed property with a bank or insurance company—rather than selling. One reason for this is that if you sell more than a couple of times you are considered a dealer, and pay tax at ordinary income rates. If you place a mortgage on your developed buildings, and then put up or refurbish another one, you pay no tax and your income is sheltered by the depreciation on the latest development. So you create a pyramid with borrowed money. If you're prudent, you create a perpetual-motion prosperity machine. Unfortunately, these incentives, plus native enthusiasm, all too often incite the professional builder to overreach. The next big crash carries him down.

Anyway, my successful developer clients, knowing of this risk, put some money in a conservative stock portfolio as a life preserver in case things went wrong. "You know, John," said one, "in the business we have a prayer. It goes like this: 'Please, God, just give me one more good bull market in real estate, and this time I won't piss it all away.'" We all chuckled. Alas, God obliged, but they pissed it all away.

Collecting Art

The two best reasons to buy a work of art are that *you know a lot about it* and that *you want to live with it.* Buying art to make money is rarely successful for the nonprofessional.

The standard slogans that one hears about investing in art seem to me to be true only for the expert. Here are some counterslogans for the nonexpert.

1. First, works of art in general do not tend to increase in value.

Specific schools or categories are always advancing, while others, former favorites, quietly fade away.

Ask a really good friend in the world of art (preferably a collector or writer on the subject, rather than a dealer) this question: If you took every single painting that was sold for the first time in, say, 1880, 1910, or 1940, and evaluated it at today's market prices, would the whole package now be worth more or less than it was then? The vast preponderance of these works will have simply vanished off the meter. They are languishing as bric-à-brac or gathering dust in attics. Even so, one could give them a "guesstimate" value. It would be low, since they would be of mediocre quality and the artists themselves would be forgotten.

Another way of asking the same question would be, Are the pictures that hung in the average Victorian house worth as much today as they were then? Of course, there would be the minuscule handful of interesting works by painters of that era (probably neglected at the time) that are still of interest today: perhaps one-tenth of 1 percent of the whole kit. Would the increase in this handful offset the depreciation in the others? Most unlikely.

I have seen a study of the prices at which Titian sold from his own time until recently. The value in constant dollars was about the same throughout the centuries. There had been no investment return, just an inflation hedge—and then only if you had successfully picked out Titian from among other painters. Another study showed that a Landseer—one of the top favorite English painters of his time—sold for £2,257 in 1875; half a century later, in 1928, it fetched a mere £38!

I suspect that the average work of art steadily declines in constant-dollar terms from the date it is first sold; but a fairer approach in a discussion of investment is to ask how it has made out in relation to investments in securities. If you reckoned a total return of 8 percent compounded on a broadly diversified stock portfolio, $1 in 1928 would have become over $100 by now, before taxes. I doubt if anyone would claim that all the works of art that changed hands in 1928 are worth on average over a hundred times now as much as they were then.

2. "Selection" will not solve the problem.

Somebody was clever enough to anticipate the importance that Renoir would have later on and to buy him cheap. His name was Dr. Barnes, of Philadelphia. But will the General Motors executive who goes around to the Hammer Gallery to sink $50,000 into a picture that he hopes will "go up" do likewise? Hardly. Those who in fact buy art successfully do so through highly skilled selection, but only professionals are likely to have that skill.

The retail buyer has to buy what is on sale retail, and the gallery business is tough enough so that the dealer can only afford to keep on his walls what is going to move fairly easily. For most of his life Renoir was not sold in the fashionable galleries. You bought his paintings from the painter directly. The wealthy collector of that day accumulated works by painters whose names have now been forgotten, and whose value today is negligible. Look at the French Prix de Rome winners between 1870 and 1900. None of their names would be known today to the nonprofessional, and I doubt if one could find more than a handful of people who would hang one of their works over the fireplace. Of course, if you went out *now*, after seventy-five or a hundred years, and picked up these efforts for a fraction of what they sold for originally (adjusting for the change in the value of the franc), you might easily do well. I do not know where you would find them. The first owner, however, would have had no return at all on his (or her) capital:

Prix de Rome

1870—Jacques Lematte	1885—Alexis Axilatte
1871—Edouard Toudouze	1886—Charles Lebayle
1872—Joseph Ferrier	1887—Henri Dauger
1873—Aimé Morot	1889—Laurent This
1874—Albert Besnard	1890—André Devambez
1875—Léon Comerre	1891—Alexander Lavelley
1876—Joseph Wencker	1892—Georges Lavergne
1877—Théobald Chartran	1893—Maurice Mitrecey
1878—Francis Schommer	1894—Jules Leroux
1879—Alfred Bramtot	1895—Antoine Larée
1880—Victor Blavette	1896—Charles Moulin
1881—Louis Fournier	1898—Amédée Gilbert
1882—Gustave Popelin	1899—Louis Roger
1883—André Basche	1900—Fernand Sabatte
1884—Henri Pinta	

No prize was awarded in 1888 or 1897, although Degas, Cézanne, Matisse, Monet, Renoir, and Toulouse-Lautrec were available!

3. You cannot ordinarily expect to discover bargains.

This applies to the nonexpert almost by definition. Books on investing in art or antiques love to describe the successful treasure hunt: The author is poking around a provincial antique store, when suddenly he perceives a broken-down armchair which, thanks to his keen eye, he recognizes as a Louis XIII original, and not, as the dealer supposes, a nineteenth-century imitation. Feigning indifference, he bargains down the price from $800 to $700 and carries off his gem. Restored, it sells for $15,000.

Or at the preview of a forthcoming auction, peering at a murky canvas with his flashlight and *loupe*, he discerns under the varnish what may be a signature. He bids the piece in for $500, carries it home, gets to work with his bottles and swabs, and presently uncovers the name of that rare master, Klaus von Obergurgl. The Cinderella of the last auction fetches $27,000 at the next one.

Here again, though, one is not talking about an investment. This activity represents a major commitment of study and time. It is a business, like prospecting for minerals. Furthermore, these books virtually never describe major coups. The best you can reasonably hope for as an outsider is a series of small gains, plus the thrill of discovery, which, to be sure, is pretty good fun. It is like the optimists you see searching beaches with metal detectors—from time to time they unearth a quarter or a tin pail, but there's no reasonable return on the time involved. And, *you're even more likely to get stuck with a fake.* The seller has had plenty of time to get—or not get—an expert authentication.

4. One should not necessarily look for the "best."

Dealers usually tell you that the "prime" object in its class—the most expensive—is the one to collect. I can see why they would take this position, since the expensive pieces occupy less space per dollar of rent. Nevertheless, a study of auction records seems to me to indicate that if a period or a school comes into favor, a "package" of secondary works may well have a bigger percentage gain than the most prominent representatives. (However, if interest dries up completely, there may well be a better chance of selling a "prime" piece at *some* price than selling a secondary one.)

5. Do not be surprised to encounter a vast amount of chicanery, "hype," and conflict of interest.

The art market resembles Wall Street in the nineteenth century. It is heavily manipulated. Some of the amazing prices you read of in auctions are created by the gallery owner selling to himself—what Wall Street calls "painting the tape." There is scarcely an uglier passage in the history of commerce than some of the transactions of that labyrinth of Liechtenstein companies called the Marlborough Gallery.

So, what does work?

Some Principles of Successful Art Investment

1. What has once been in fashion will again be in fashion.

A number of successful collectors I've known have followed this principle.

One college friend of mine, Cary Welch, became fond of Moghul miniatures in the 1950s, when few collectors were interested in them, and now has a famous and valuable collection. A second was entranced by early American folk paintings at a time when good examples cost $10 or $15. A third, Nikita Lobanov, excited by the Diaghilev phenomenon, bought important ballet set and costume designs from the widows and ex-mistresses of the artists who worked for Diaghilev. A Boston friend responded to the harsh glamour of the clipper-ship era and formed an outstanding collection of ship paintings at a time when they could be had for $100 each. An English friend, Sir Leon Bagrit, bought Renaissance bronzes in the 1930s, when they were out of vogue, eventually developing a notable collection, and another London merchant banker friend did the same with medieval coins.

The common thread here is that in each case there is a profound authenticity about the objects, and a real fondness for them on the part of the collector. In most instances the buyers became extremely knowledgeable in their fields. Several in due course began buying directly from the owners, since at the time the dealers did not find the category sufficiently interesting to carry.

I once developed a theory that depression-era WPA art had to be as far out of vogue as it could get, and made inquiries. I found a huge cache in a warehouse on Staten Island, owned by a plumbing contractor who used the canvases to wrap pipes. He would sell the works in 100-pound lots; you paid a premium if you insisted on selecting what you got.

By the 1960s, Hudson River school painters of the "Stag at Eve" type had gone out of style in an era of Plexiglas, chrome, and geometric prints. Then, in the late 1970s, they advanced spectacularly. For that matter, my nineteenth-century Prix de Rome winners, along with religious art, hit bottom a while back.

An example from my own enthusiasms is the nineteenth-century French *animalier* sculptors: the two Baryes, Mêne, Rosa and Isidore Bonheur, and the rest. I'm fond of the better ones, and suspect that almost anybody would be too if he just kept a representative work on his desk where he could look at it by itself. In Europe, these works were produced in large editions and brought excellent prices about a hundred years ago. Then they fell into eclipse, and by World War II were often used as doorstops or even melted down for their metal content. Priced at $50 to $75 for a good piece in the 1950s, they have now mounted to several thousand dollars.

2. Buy crafts that become accepted as minor arts.

It may be that the safest things to collect for profit are pleasing objects on the borderline between craft and art that are made honestly and carefully, express the feelings of the people of a particular era, and have artistic merit, but that are not yet fully recognized as art. Examples from my own observation include American quilts, primitive folk paintings and ship portraits, or, at one time, the "floating world" prints, some of which the Japanese used as wrapping paper. My Japanese housekeeper received from her brother a set of Hokusai's *Thirty-six Views of Mount Fuji* at a time when they had little value. She gave some away in the 1960s when they were selling for $40 or so. Recently she found they were going for thousands of dollars each. Currier and Ives prints have had a similar revaluation in the last generation or two. So have scrimshaw and glass paperweights. I've watched *vues d'optique* rise tenfold since I first bought a number. A Mexican associate of mine, Antonio Haas, used to send his friends the appealing little crude votive oil paintings on tin sheets that peasants left in churches, which cost about 35 cents at the time. Now they sell for hundreds of dollars, and he has none himself. My own collection of illustrated "clipper cards"—in essence, advertising flyers—were originally distributed gratis by the shipowners. I used to get them for $100 or so; now they cost in the low thousands.

At the time they are attractive buys, such objects are not yet carried by art dealers, reposing instead in thrift shops, junk stores, and flea markets. The class of object in question is regarded as plentiful enough to be cast off without thought or stuck in the attic.

3. When a country gets rich, it buys back its own history.

Another principle that works well is collecting prime examples of the art of countries that are destined to thrive economically. For instance, after World War II, when everybody was poor except the United States, there was a boom in U.S. furniture and painting. The the prosperous Japanese bid up the Oriental pieces, followed by a boom in Islamic art as the oil-rich Middle Easterners bought back their national treasures. Chinese, Korean, Taiwanese, and Eastern European pieces are following the same course. Since the Cuban economic straitjacket can scarcely survive its "maximum leader" Castro, Cuban art should be an interesting bet.

Some Hazards

For any specific object there may well be no satisfactory market when you want to sell it. If you buy during a period when it is in vogue, you may have to wait until the wheel comes around again. And even then, a "round trip" at an auction gallery costs about 40 percent, and at a dealer's at least 50 percent, often more. Add the sales tax, and you can reckon that a complete transaction may well cost over 60 percent. That is a severe handicap to overcome. (A round trip in ATT, by contrast, costs about 1 percent, plus tax.)

Then too, almost everything in art can be—and is—forged. There are entire forgery factories in Italy, Russia, and other countries, and inevitably, organized crime has entered the business. *So never buy an important piece without a certificate of authenticity from an impeccable outside authority.*

Gold and Precious Stones

Gold is just what you need during great upheavals and runaway inflation. Europeans usually have a stash somewhere, and it is almost the basic form of wealth for women in India. It is universally accepted, so you can sell a coin or two in a hurry if you need to; it is valuable, so an amount you can carry will keep you going for a long time; it doesn't tarnish, is readily malleable, and easy to assay.

But in ordinary times it is less useful. Almost all the gold ever produced is still around, and at a price it emerges on the market. You can't have a "squeeze," since the supply is all but infinite. Thus, *you shouldn't calculate the gold outlook on a supply-demand basis, like an industrial mineral such as copper,* whose supply has to roughly follow demand.

Rather, gold is a speculative football. Every now and again it takes off on a move that continues for several years as speculators pile in. Then the bubble collapses.

Gold-mining *stocks* are a bit different. They constitute a market group, which from time to time comes to life like any other group. Toward the top of a speculative bubble in the metal, investors start doing euphoric calculations of future mining profits, and the stocks soar. Then matters get back to a normal basis.

As to precious stones, if you buy a diamond or colored stone at Harry Winston and trot it across Fifth Avenue to Cartier's to sell it again, you will do well to get 60 percent of what you just paid, minus tax. So *precious stones are a field for specialists.*

And you can get caught by changing vogues. The very building in which Cartier's is housed was swapped to Pierre Cartier by a rich family called Plant for one pearl necklace. Then came cultured pearls, and the market changed forever.

Diamonds are a bet *against* synthetic stones, and *for* the continuation of the De Beers monopoly, whose Consolidated Selling Organization actually benefits everybody, unlike any other monopoly, since we all prefer our diamond heirlooms to remain valuable. I do not know which factor will prevail.

Gemstones, unlike gold, are individual, subjectively appraised, and not negotiable in small amounts, so they do not seem to me to constitute a convenient store of value.

One Way to Get Rich

Step number one is to abandon the respectable East Coast point of view. Very few of my "successful" friends in the East are getting *rich*: They either started out that way or else just have good jobs, as law partners, Wall Street types, company presidents or vice-presidents, or whatever. These friends of mine do become respectable; but after taxes only a handful make it really big, the way people did in the old days or still do in places like Mexico, Brazil, Thailand, Korea, or Taiwan, with palaces in town, yachts, ranches here and there, and collections they eventually give to museums. To get rich you should think like an Elizabethan, an adventurer; like the American of a century ago, not his clerkish descendant of today. You should decide to become a builder of wealth, not a curator.

Second, you should ask yourself: Where am I needed enough so that I can really get paid for it if I'm able to stand some risk and discomfort? One good answer is: in the developing countries with idle resources. If you are sufficiently clever and energetic enough to make the grade in a good law firm, you probably have what it takes to play a role in building up a developing country.

In such places it is taken for granted that one works hard, takes risks, creates something, and is well rewarded for it. American friends of mine have started a chain of restaurants and one of photo stores in Hungary, both with multi-hundred-million-dollar market capitalizations, planted vineyards in Australia, developed a minerals empire in British Columbia, created the principal agricultural-equipment distribution company in Central America, organized the Hong Kong television station, started a bottling company in Thailand, developed a large petrochemical complex in southern Spain, organized an investment bank in Madrid, put together a fertilizer complex in Korea, and started the Levi's company in Greece. I can cite hundreds of such cases, and indeed have done a few myself. These people live magnificently, with swarms of servants who are delighted to have the work. They're merchant princes. That also gives them a chance to exercise a benevolent influence if they're so inclined: To give the public the Morgan Library or the Frick Collection, the founders first had to make the money.

Here is the actual process. First, you should know something valuable before you set off. A good grasp of mutual fund sales, or consumer merchandising, or investment banking (the "deal business") may do it, or a degree in engineering plus a few years operating in a telecommunications company, or field and money-raising experience in oil or hard-rock geology, or a thorough knowledge of consumer credit or leasing, or of a consumer business, such as bottling or mail-order. You must have a business sense, entrepreneurial flair, a taste for exotic food and languages. You also need six months' or a year's eating money, preferably borrowed from older family members.

After you arrive in Saigon, Santiago, São Paolo, Sydney, Singapore, or San José (a free-enterprise orientation and a high growth rate being indispensable), ask around about the young Americans who are doing interesting things. Visit them. Call on the leading banks and lawyers (preferably with letters of introduction from your own) and take soundings. Everybody will give you lunch and make suggestions. Write it all down. Visit the local development bank and whatever the ministry of development is called, and the people who run the local and the American chambers of commerce.

If you push right along following up leads, within a couple of months you will have found three or four projects in search of an entrepreneur, including, with luck, one or two where your expertise is applicable. There will be a top fast-food or car rental franchise available, for instance; or a group will want to put up a specialty chemical plant or open a mine and doesn't know the correct foreign know-how partner; or the local beer tastes terrible and investors would be glad to put money into a joint venture with a foreign beer company, but they don't know which one; or a hotel site is available but Hilton has said no . . . who should be next? The development bank manager can tell you of a dozen such projects that look good but which he is too busy to do more than lend to when they mature. A good start for many projects is finding a foreign brand-name product that needs distribution locally. You get it established in the market, and then by degrees move into manufacturing it on the spot.

In a couple of months you will have five telephone calls waiting for you whenever you get back to your hotel, and after two or three months more you can decide to work on two or three of these projects for a piece of the action and expenses—but no salary.

If you are always honest, energetic, and careful, then even if the first project doesn't score, you will get a reputation for being serious, and after a while the solid groups will seek you out with something really worthwhile.

The obvious function for the technically competent young American in this situation is writing the feasibility study in English, using a variety of assumptions and with the figures fully worked out, and then helping find the foreign know-how or capital partner. When you have got the study in adequate form, go home and ask the uncle who grub-staked you for suggestions. He or one of his cronies in a management consulting firm will give you introductions to three or four companies. Present the deal to the most likely company last. The first presentations may reveal distressing shortcomings in your feasibility study. By the last one, though, you should have thought of almost everything.

It's easier to put this sort of thing together than you'd think. Have yourself cut in for a free 5 percent interest and a part-time job as assistant managing director. After two or three years and a couple of small projects ($1 or $2 million or so), you can try for the brass ring of a $10 million hotel or bottling company or a $20 million manufacturing plant. If you promote it from scratch, you can deal yourself in for quite a lot of free stock, and you'll be on your way.

All this can be done in the United States, where we have our own frontiers in the sense of growth industries, but the competition is much tougher. Large corporations are constantly sifting through stacks of expansion possibilities. There are competent dealmakers even in provincial centers. And in the United States you haven't got the comfortable margin for error that you have in a developing country, where there are more opportunities, less competing talent, and a chance to look up the answers in the back of the book, so to speak, by bringing in existing foreign business ideas and technology.

Anyway, it only takes one 5 or 10 percent free slice of a large project and you are off to the races. If the enterprise succeeds and after five or ten years is worth three or four times as much, you've made it. The chances may be better than you think, although by no means certain: I have other adventurer friends who went to the wrong countries or who weren't all that able and who haven't become tycoons, or even successful. But even they seem to me to exude a sense of a life more fully experienced than most of my country-club professional acquaintances, and above all, their careers have been *useful*.

I am not talking about putting money into foreign ventures without going there. It will be lost. I am talking about going and *staying*, about committing your early working life to a place that needs your energy, talent, and knowledge of a more advanced economy, and will reward it handsomely. No one can guarantee that this prescription will make you rich, but it probably won't happen any other way.

I'm also involved with a number of pro bono activities in the developing world, and can say with confidence that skilled entrepreneurs are far more needed there than social workers. They also have more fun. As Learned Hand puts it, ". . . in establishing a business, or in excavating an ancient city, or in rearing a family, or in writing a play . . . in all chosen jobs the craftsman must be at work, and the craftsman, as Stevenson says, gets his hire as he goes. . . . If it be selfishness to work on the job one likes, because one likes it and for no other end, let us accept the odium."

PART 4

Planning Your Finances

How Much Can I Live On?

Never sell Consols," canny trustee Soames Forsyte used to caution his heirs, in the Galsworthy novels. Consols were the long-term British government bonds that the English had in mind when in former times they would say of a person of property: "He has ten thousand a year." Before World War I that sum, in pounds, gave you a very good living indeed, since *inflation and tax were no problem then.* But alas, if the *Forsyte Saga* descendants had followed Soames's advice, they would now be wiped out. As a result of inflation, long-term British bonds of the World War I era are now worth in real terms only 1 percent or so of their value then. In addition, the income has been put through a ferocious tax wringer.

The "rule of 72" tells you how fast money doubles at compound interest. It's the interest rate divided into 72. So at 12 percent, for instance, your $100,000 becomes $200,000 in six years. The rule also works in reverse. Money loses half its real value in the number of years that the inflation rate goes into 72. Thus, in a time of 6 percent inflation, the half-life of money is twelve years. So in just twenty-five years of 6 percent inflation, the bonds in a portfolio will have been cut in half twice, or be worth in real terms a quarter of what they were at the outset; in fifty years they will be worth a sixteenth. In other words, the bond component of a portfolio will essentially have been boiled away.

With hindsight, we can see that a young Forsyte who in 1910 had a fixed income of £10,000 a year and wanted to maintain his standard of living needed to put at least half his income from Consols into an inflation replacement fund, and only live on the remaining half, after taxes.

Then let's take the opposite case. Those who bought Berkshire Hathaway, Warren Buffett's vehicle, when I made it the lead study in *The Money Masters* fifteen years ago, by today have made 100 percent a year (simple interest) on their investment, while receiving no income at all. So nominal income is not the whole story. It requires some analysis and adjustment before you can with confidence establish the standard of living you will be able to sustain.

When discussing budgets with a new client, I first point out that, like a military commander, *you must have reserves*. Your Treasury bills and gold are your cavalry over the hill, which you may need to save the day when the battle goes against you: your lifeboat, your parachute. They aren't there to enable you to sail faster or fly higher, just to save your neck. (Of course, if during a washout you have the nerve to commit your reserves successfully, like Wellington at Waterloo and the British Rothschilds just afterwards, then you can make a tremendous killing.)

Now, let's be specific. Suppose a recently retired couple has an income of $100,000 from investments. And suppose they keep a quarter of their capital in liquid reserves—mostly bonds. The 6 percent interest (let's say) that they collect from those reserves is not truly spendable income, since the value of the bonds in real terms—even assuming quite a low inflation rate—is declining about as fast after tax as the interest is being paid. So if our couple has an income of $100,000, of which some $25,000 comes from bonds, the realistic course is to add almost all of that $25,000 back to capital and only start the budget calculation with the remaining $75,000.

But that $75,000 may again be truly spendable or not, depending on how it's generated. If it represents the income from a portfolio of utility stocks whose dividends barely rise each year, or if the companies are maintaining their dividend increases by adding to long-term debt, then the couple is potentially in the situation of our 1910 Englishman. They should conceptually also put aside a substantial part of their stock income as an income replacement fund.

If, on the contrary, the $75,000 represents the yield from a portfolio of high-growth stocks with low dividends, then the couple can spend somewhat more than their after-tax dividends and still be gaining in real terms. With a portfolio invested in outstanding enterprises like 3M, American International Group, or indeed Berkshire Hathaway, one can spend more than the current dividend. Suppose the yield on these stocks is 3 percent, and the dividends are rising at 10 percent a year. On that basis, spending 5 percent a year, say, of the then capital value should work out. (3M reinvests half of its earnings for further growth, American International Group 90%, and Berkshire 100%.) And since a portfolio of growth stocks with rising dividends yields more, after some years, than a portfolio of income stocks, the situation gets better and better. Of course, you have to be careful and realistic in following this policy, but so must you be in following a high-income strategy. Bonds can get into trouble, and dividends can be disappointing.

If the portfolio is made up of old first-tier greats—Eastman Kodak, General Eiectric, Gillette, Johnson & Johnson, and the like—then one can probably spend roughly the full amount (but not more) of the dividends in reasonable confidence that their current yield will in due course rise in line with inflation.

Another point: When I point out to retired persons—who because of the "money illusion" of unreal income are spending more than they really should—the risk of running low and ending up in straitened circumstances in their late seventies, they often say, "Well, I don't expect to live that long." Quite the contrary! Many well-off persons make it into their late eighties. Nothing prolongs life like a comfortable income, particularly, I seem to observe, if there's a pack of hungry heirs that are being kept waiting indefinitely. So be realistic and conservative. Let the surprises be pleasant ones.

Here are two examples from my own experience. A widow I'll call Ellen Paulson was left a substantial amount of money by her husband when he died. The income went to her for life, with the capital to be divided among their three children after her death. Her late husband had been a successful New York businessman, and the family had two comfortable houses: one in Greenwich, Connecticut, and one on Cape Cod, where they went in summer. The children liked coming to the Greenwich place on weekends and spending long periods on Cape Cod in summer, so she kept both. In consequence, as the years went by Mrs. Paulson found herself living at the limit of her resources.

At her annual meeting with her trustees, the problem was aired frankly. How could she maintain the houses and keep up roughly the same standard of living as before, with her husband's considerable salary no longer available? Every year or two it was decided to sell some growth stocks with low yields and move into bonds or high-yielding equities to maintain the needed income, in the hope that all would be well.

So the trust portfolio eventually became roughly half fixed-income securities and half high-dividend stocks, notably utilities and the like.

Unfortunately, however, the investment objective was impossible on its face. At that time her costs were rising 8 percent a year, so in order to stay even in real terms, her income had to rise 12 to 15 percent, since her tax bracket was also rising. Now, very few income stocks increase their dividends at anything like 15 percent a year; and, of course, bond payments don't increase at all.

After some fifteen years of a princely existence, Ellen Paulson's buying power in real terms was about 40 percent of what it had been just after her husband died. The old trustees, friends of her husband, stepped down, and new ones with a more austere and realistic attitude came in. They were dismayed at what they saw. She had to sell both her houses and move into a smaller one, where it was a strain to have her children for weekends, since they now had families of their own and came in groups of four or five.

Mrs. Paulson has many years of life ahead of her, which she will spend in straitened circumstances. If she had cut back right away and adopted a realistic investment policy, she could have been comfortable for her lifetime.

Furthermore, when in the future the children come into their shrunken inheritance, they will have a justifiable complaint against the old trustees, if they're still around. They can't make out a case at law, but they can certainly make one on the basis of common sense. By investing flat out for income in a time of inflation, the trustees knowingly dissipated the corpus of the testator's estate. When the children ask what happened to their inheritance, their elders will have to explain that it was essentially blown on high living. In fact, Ellen herself also has a reasonable complaint. The original trustees, as old business friends of her husband, were paid to give her the benefit of their realism and experience. Why didn't they look ahead and set her on a sustainable course?

One time a lawyer acquaintance got in touch to say he had a client who might need our services. The client was a thirty-four-year-old mason I'll call Will Black, who had been working on scaffolding outside a house in suburban Philadelphia. The scaffolding had given way and he fell onto the stone terrace below. After a year in the hospital, he was still unable to walk. Litigation ensued, and he eventually collected an award of $1,200,000, of which the lawyer got a third. So Black found himself confined to a wheelchair, with $800,000 to keep him going for life.

At a conference with Black, his wife, and the lawyer (I'll call him Bingham), I was handed the portfolio, which was in corporate and municipal bonds, including some junk bonds, and a money fund.

Black was cheerful enough, and his young wife, snappily turned out, seemed on the crest of the wave. "Mr. Bingham has arranged for us to get an income of $4,500 a month," she said. "That's more than twice what Will got when he was working. We've had to spend a lot to remodel our house, putting in ramps and a swimming pool that Will can work out in, but even then we're doing fine. We were thinking of renting a place in Florida for the winters—just a little place."

My mind wasn't on Florida. "But why did you put the whole portfolio into bonds?" I asked. The young wife replied: "It's more conservative. I wouldn't want to spend more than our income. So Mr. Bingham suggested bonds. This way, even after taxes, we're living within our means."

I gave the lawyer a long look. It was time to explain the "money illusion" to the group. By spending all their income, the Blacks were in real terms dipping heavily into capital, since the true value of the bond portfolio was declining every year because of inflation. At that rate, they would be down to half their present standard of living in fifteen years, and to a quarter in another fifteen. They would be in a pickle.

"Unless you think inflation's going to stop, under your present strategy, you'll be impoverished sooner or later," I said. "The only question is when. These days, I'd say that a prudent level of expenditure would be 5 percent or so of your capital, *if you're invested in assets that will increase in value as fast as inflation*. So you should move by degrees into stocks, buying when the market is weak, and do a new budget based on spending about $3,000 a month, minus taxes, but rising as the cost of living rises."

"Isn't investing in stocks risky?" Mrs. Black wanted to know.

I nodded. "Not too risky, I hope."

"But some conserve stocks yield 6 percent," said Bingham. "Some of the utilities . . ."

"I'm sorry to be discouraging," I said, "but in general their dividends are no longer rising as fast as inflation. They sound conservative, because they're old, well-known names, but they may not do the job of preserving capital."

Will Black, who struck me as a stouthearted fellow, accepted all this and even seemed relieved. He must have sensed that the lawyer's plan was extravagant, even though his wife liked it. Goodbye to some of those luxuries. Mr. Bingham looked sheepish. We set a new meeting date.

But even "conservative" stocks aren't necessarily the answer. You have to try a bit harder than that. As older readers will remember, after World War II a typical trust portfolio looked something like this, and paid a good yield: U.S. Treasury bonds, corporate bonds, municipal bonds, Alcoa, AT&T, Cleveland Electric, Du Pont, General Motors, Owens-Illinois, Pennsylvania Railroad, Texaco, Westinghouse Electric, U.S. Gypsum, and U.S. Steel.

Where were these "conservative investments" a quarter of a century later? Let's assume an original principal of $100,000. Assume further that half of the principal was in bonds—as was usual then—and that the bonds were rolled over every ten years. After twenty-five years, the portfolio had a market value of about $117,000. In purchasing power, that was about $36,000—a loss of 64 percent in real dollars. Safe? Conservative?

"Conservative" investing tends to produce a portfolio with too many mature, slow-growth companies, throttled by restrictive unions, fierce competition, consumerism, and hostile regulation, and which have trouble attracting top young executives. So a familiar name is not necessarily conservative at all. Rather, it is a security blanket that may not keep you warm.

Insurance: A Gambling Game Where the Odds Favor the House

Harvard's great treasurer Paul Cabot once told me: "I don't understand a goddamn thing about insurance, except that I don't want to have any." By this typically crusty utterance he meant that although insurance is necessary in certain situations, it is not a good deal from an investment standpoint. It is very specifically a gambling game, and was originally so regulated. Other than the obvious emergency requirements, notably third-party disability, Major Medical, and homeowner's, the chief need for insurance in an investment plan is to take care of the family if the breadwinner dies before there is enough capital laid by to handle necessities, such as children's education. For this, term life is a precise and efficient solution. The investment or "endowment" component of ordinary or whole life is over long periods not nearly as satisfactory a way of building as more conventional investments.

Let's go a bit more into when you really *do* need insurance.

Three insurable disasters can rock your financial security: a big liability suit; a catastrophic illness; or a fire in your home that isn't properly covered. As to the last, your homeowner's insurance ordinarily only covers your home fully if it is set at no less than 80 percent of the structure's *replacement* value (not cost, not market; and of course the grounds needn't be included). So it's dangerous to underinsure. (*Over*insuring—e.g., an expensive car at its purchase price of some years back—is a bad joke on you. The company will happily pocket the excessive premiums for all those years, but when the time comes to pay off after a loss, a flinty adjuster appears, who refuses to pay more than the then Blue Book value of a similar used vehicle.)

A big liability suit can clean you out: Even the lawyers' bills can be excruciatingly expensive. So, get the largest umbrella policy available—$5 million being a usual limit these days. That way the insurance company takes over right away and fights the case in court.

Not having appropriate Major Medical can ruin everything in the event of a catastrophe. *Here the key thing is to make sure you're protected against inflation*, and that the "interior limits" are reasonable. Many company group policies are convertible to individual policies that you can take with you when you leave the company. Indeed, this is mandated under a number of states' laws. However, when you do leave, the converted policy usually offers inferior coverage, and may not protect you from inflation. *Talk to your company treasurer about this: Maybe you can improve your situation*. There are a few individual policies one can buy before age sixty-five that become good Medicare supplements after retirement, although many insurance companies no longer offer them. A number of companies offer good Medicare supplemental plans for people sixty-five and over that cover the reasonable cost of doctors' services not paid for by Medicare, plus varying degrees of nursing care. Coverage of prescription drugs is limited, at best. (The American Association of Retired Persons—which you can join at age fifty-five—has deals with mail-order drugstores that greatly reduce pharmaceutical costs.) Nursing home policies exist, but are rarely satisfactory. (Of course, all these principles will require restudy after the proposed national health plan goes into effect.)

Cut down on insurance you don't absolutely require, such as car collision, and elect the highest deductibles you can afford. Remember, *insurance is a gambling game where the odds favor the house*. So get only what's essential, but be sure you get that.

Elderly people often buy an apartment in a "life care" community where you live more or less normally while you are in good health, but where you are entitled to full medical care if you fall ill. This can be an interesting variation of the insurance principle.

Here's some very important advice: *Every year have your insurance broker send you "a schedule of insurance in force"* showing what you have, *with suggestions. Be sure he really thinks things out*. Often one kind of insurance overlaps another, and often there are serious gaps.

Consider a Prenuptial Agreement

People often think that a prenuptial agreement only makes sense for very rich couples who want to guard against one of them trying to grab the other's money if they split up. Not so! Many couples should consider a prenuptial agreement, as is common among the well-to-do in Europe. It's a touchy subject in a first marriage, unless one spouse has significantly more property than the other, but easy in a second marriage. I find that a good way to start things off is to suggest that the couple needs at least to agree on what happens if one of them should die.

One should think of a "prenup" like a will.* You can of course die without a will, leaving the distribution of your estate to probate law, but no prudent person does. Similarly, it's often better for a couple to decide property issues in a cool, rational frame of mind rather than in the emotional tumult of separation.

Here are some other advantages:

1. *Control.* Such an agreement gives the parties what they and their advisors agree they want, not what politicos in each state have decided they ought to want.

2. *Limiting creditor claims.* Creditors in a bankruptcy will lunge for everything in sight. A spouse's assets can be protected by establishing them as separate in a prenuptial agreement.

---

* Incidentally, one good way to insulate inherited assets from the claims of a disaffected spouse—and creditors—is to bequeath them in trust, even a trust so broad that it almost corresponds to outright ownership.

3. *Preventing disruption of a partnership.* Part of the value in a business partnership may be considered "marital property," subject to division with everything else. A partnership agreement often requires that the individual partners obtain prenuptial (or, if it's still possible, postnuptial) agreements exempting partnership interests from such a settlement. Otherwise the firm may find itself caught up in a squabble over valuation, perhaps having to buy out a partner's interest that has been taken over by the partner's ex.

4. *Limiting estate claims.* Ordinarily, a surviving spouse can claim part of the deceased spouse's estate. (This right was once limited to real estate and called the right of *dower* for a woman and *courtesy* for a man.) It may be appropriate to ask a spouse to waive or modify this claim. That can be done, since prenuptial agreements supersede both inheritance and "right of election" laws.

5. *Children.* Having a second spouse limit or waive claims on property, gifts, or inheritance may be necessary to protect the rights of children by a previous marriage, not only from unfair property dispositions but also from the hatred and strain engendered by litigation.

6. *Unequal opportunity.* The Equal Opportunity principle often works against divorced women. The law presumes they can compete on equal terms in the job market, but in reality women quite often dedicate what would have been their early professional years to supporting a husband's career and raising a family. So in practice a woman may face a greatly reduced standard of living once she's on her own. It's deplorable but not that rare for a successful professional or businessman to divorce the wife who slaved to get him through medical, law, or business school in favor of a younger colleague. And his business can only be valued as of the trial date, even though it thrives thereafter. "Equal Opportunity" isn't nearly enough for the abandoned wife in such a situation. She deserves much better, and could well try to establish it from the first.

So, in essence, a prenuptial agreement lets a couple take charge of their own destiny by establishing their mutual wishes on unshuffling their property should the marriage not work, or when a spouse dies. The parties are applying their own judgment to their particular circumstances rather than relying on the accidents of state jurisprudence. Although trial judges are held to the state's general legal principles, beyond that they have wide discretion. You just don't know what they'll do.

A court will usually sustain a "prenup" agreement over state law if it seems well considered and reasonably equitable. Such an agreement means less complicated, bitter, and expensive divorce proceedings, if it comes to that. Divorce litigation is horrible and humiliating. An engaged couple may feel that state law has to be fair and should therefore govern; but how do they reconcile that idea with the existence of quite different laws in different states? And a couple may very well move from the state where they got married to another with an altogether different family law regime. *Both* can't represent a monopoly of divine wisdom! A prenup can specify that a particular state's laws will govern even if the couple change their domicile.

For instance, if you get divorced in California without a prenuptial agreement, you may discover with horror that *everything* acquired during a marriage, except by inheritance, is considered to be owned fiftyfifty. Your rare book collection would be viewed as half-owned by your spouse. There are nine of these "community property" states: Arkansas, California, Idaho, Louisiana, Nevada, New Mexico, Texas, Washington, and Wisconsin. Untangling illiquid assets to produce exact equality is obviously difficult and may result in breaking up collections and selling off cherished heirlooms. I have more than once encountered instances of an angry departing wife successfully capturing her husband's family memorabilia and even golf trophies—things you'd think she didn't want to see any more of.

Most of the other states follow the "equitable distribution" principle. In general, *earnings* during the marriage are divided, particularly earnings in which the other spouse had any role. In some states, including Connecticut, both inherited property and property acquired before the marriage are subject to equitable distribution. Since the court is not held to a fifty-fifty split as in a community property state, an equitable distribution state may be a better deal for a spouse with much more capital than the other.

However, the settlement process is likely to be painful, prolonged, and expensive, and the outcome unpredictable. Very often indeed, warring couples sitting in a conference room listening to lawyers squabble—and run up huge bills—wish they'd had a prenuptial agreement. It also often makes sense to write a *post*nuptial agreement, after the couple understand their needs, even if they are on the best of terms.

In this area, *you must seek advice from a matrimonial law specialist, not a general lawyer*. There are tax issues. And if you have more than one residence, or are married to a foreigner, there may be jurisdictional issues. For instance, France will accept jurisdiction in a matrimonial case involving a French national who got married and has thereafter always lived in the United States. And the agreement must be drafted to withstand attack: Courts can set aside agreements signed under duress or when the settlement is unfairly skewed, when there was fraud or incomplete disclosure of financial assets and liabilities, or when either party did not have independent counsel. So it takes a specialized attorney to walk you through all these issues and make sure the deal is tight.

Investing for Retirement:
Start Early!

Here are some suggestions based on hundreds of family situations I have worked with. Please consider them hints, rather than specific recommendations. For a detailed analysis, you need tailormade suggestions from a specialized professional advisor: not a generalist lawyer, accountant, or insurance broker, but a trust and estate specialist. Throughout, though, runs one key principle: *Start early*. The government yearns to levy a huge tax on your estate. To avoid that you should plan way in advance, particularly as to gifts to later generations. So I'll say it again: *Start early*.

Inflation-Proof Your Retirement Capital

These days one tends to live for a long time after reaching retirement age. Providing for one's postretirement years is thus a much bigger problem than it once was. An elderly couple often has to subsist for twenty or twenty-five years on whatever the breadwinner has been able to put aside. The annoying thing is that except for federal employees, who enjoy indexed pensions, there is no longer a simple, neat solution. "Safe as houses," one used to say . . . before rent control. Farms were a nice, safe asset once: all gone now! In the old days of very low inflation, people used to refer to wealth in terms of income: "She has £3,000 a year," they say in the novels of Jane Austen. Today, the purchasing power of any given sum will shrink drastically during the period of one's retirement. Older readers will remember the series of ads run for years by an annuity company in such publications as *Life*

Magazine: A cheerful-looking couple are standing in front of a pleasant, modest sunny house. Underneath, the caption says: "How we retired to Florida on $250 a month." Inflation was starting to get going in earnest about that time, so a couple of years later the caption read: "How We Retired to Florida on $300 a Month." A few years later it went to $400, then $500, and then finally this ad was seen no more. I do not envy the cheerful couple. They are financially extinct—together, indeed, with the conception of the nonindexed annuity.

Between the time when those ads were appearing and today, any given amount of money has lost a good three-quarters of its value, and in many sectors nine-tenths or more. Alas for the five-cent subway ride and the ten-cent shoeshine!

So the first rule of retirement is that your plan won't work unless it is proof against inflation.

There Is Nothing in the World Like Compound Interest

The area I know best, building capital by holding financial assets for the long term, is one good solution to this problem. Looking back over the same period of four decades, and indeed for longer than that, one finds that owning shares in a number of large, solid-growing businesses provided the long-term investor with a return of around 10 percent per annum, before inflation and applicable taxes. It was higher if you did not buy the famous Dow Jones kind of stock, but rather looked for somewhat smaller, faster-growing companies. Suppose, in any event, that a program of buying stocks to build a retirement fund returns you 10 percent, before inflation and tax. Over a forty-year span it grows forty-five-fold; or twenty-two-fold if you drop the assumption to 8 percent compounded. Even cut back to reflect uncertainties, that's a lot of money. Here is a remarkable illustration of the power of compounding if you start early:

Assume that you save $2,000 a year for only eight years from ages nineteen and twenty-six. You then stop. You never pay another nickel into the fund, you just keep the money quietly growing at 10 percent compounded. You end up at retirement with more than $1 million— always before inflation and tax.

Most investors start later, are not absolutely systematic, and, just as in following a diet, for one reason or another break the flow. It follows—and this corresponds to my own observation in dealing with clients—that one should strive above all for *consistent* superior investment performance, rather than amazing performance. Swinging for

PENSIONER'S PROGRESS

Age	Contribution	Year-end Value
19	$2,000	2,200
20	2,000	4,620
21	2,000	7,282
22	2,000	10,210
23	2,000	13,431
24	2,000	16,974
25	2,000	20,872
26	2,000	25,159
27	0	27,675
28	0	30,442
29	0	33,487
30	0	36,835
31	0	40,519
32	0	44,571
33	0	49,028
34	0	53,930
35	0	59,323
36	0	65,256
37	0	71,781
38	0	78,960
39	0	86,856
40	0	95,095
41	0	105,095
42	0	115,605
43	0	127,165
44	0	139,882
45	0	153,870
46	0	169,257
47	0	186,183
48	0	204,801
49	0	225,281
50	0	247,809
51	0	272,590
52	0	299,849
53	0	329,834
54	0	362,817
55	0	399,099
56	0	439,009
57	0	482,910
58	0	531,201
59	0	584,321
60	0	642,753
61	0	707,028
62	0	777,731
63	0	855,504
64	0	941,054
65	0	1,035,160

the fences with exciting speculations is all too likely to result in a series of ups and downs that may well rupture the process, and at worst may discourage you from carrying on at all.

How to Do It

I find that the easiest philosophy likely to be executed successfully by most people is simply putting aside a fixed percentage of one's earnings—5 percent or 10 percent, let us say—to be invested every year in stocks (not bonds) for one's retirement. (In a way, as long as you are still working, you are your own bond portfolio.) This is called *dollar averaging*, and it works. Often it is done automatically by one's company pension plan, of course.

Own Your Own Home

First, our tax system encourages it. Here's why: Suppose that instead of buying, you put the price of your house into securities, and use the income to pay rent. You'll have to pay tax on the income stream (and indeed the landlord will be paying tax on the rent you pay him). So owning the house you live in is a highly tax-efficient transaction. Also, mortgage interest is generally tax-deductible. So, not only are you building an essential asset, you're getting a tax break in the process. And there's an even more important reason: inflation and indeed hyperinflation, plus very high tax brackets, come along from time to time. So you can find yourself unable to pay the rent on your home, after tax. Thus, a key rule of financing your retirement, after starting the savings habit early, is owning the place where you live. Here's a simple rule-of-thumb answer to a question one hears often, namely, whether it's a good time to buy an apartment. Over and over I've found that *you don't go far wrong buying an apartment at well below what it would cost to build it again*, which a contractor can help you estimate. And from time to time apartments do fall well below their reproduction cost: just be patient!

Second Homes

A vacation home can be a remarkably useful component of a retirement plan. I spend the summer on the coast of Maine. It's surprising how many summer houses in my neighborhood that were bought for very little have been winterized and turned into year-round residences by retired persons. The owners head off toward southern climes in winter and go on trips, but find that the quieter life of the provinces suits them well in their latter years. If that's the pattern that your life takes, then you may choose to sell your old principal residence, which by that time may have become extremely valuable, and live in your country place.

Set Up a GRIT While You Still Can

There's still another thing about a house as an asset: It offers a unique estate-tax break. Perhaps the very best estate-tax shelter still surviving is the qualified personal residence trust, or residential GRIT, which I describe in a later chapter. You can get both your primary and secondary residences entirely out of your estate, while continuing to live in them.

Which Pocket?

The various tax-sheltered retirement options that exist—401-Ks, Keoghs, IRAs, and the rest—change regularly. Get periodic advice from a specialized consultant. I do notice a fallacy in many savers' use of these plans. They hold low-yield growth stocks in a tax-sheltered retirement plan, while keeping CDs, Treasury bills, and other high-income items in their own portfolio, reasoning that they may need money in a hurry for something, and can use the income for day-to-day expenses.

To me this is illogical *for the money you are holding for retirement*. (You do of course need liquid assets for emergencies and surprises.) A family should think of each of its assets as falling somewhere along a spectrum—from the most liquid and secure to the riskiest and least liquid. There is a place for the whole range. Within this spectrum you also have different tax treatments, such as the income-tax breaks for municipal bonds, and the lack of tax, as a practical matter, on Grandma's diamond necklace.* Think of all these different tax and liquidity categories as different pockets in a suit: you have a tax-free pocket, a fully taxable pocket, and categories in between.

Now, the logical place to put the high-income items is of course in the tax-free pocket, where all the income can accumulate and be re-

---

* Leviticus, I note with interest, utters a horrible curse on whoever seeks to tax a widow's matrimonial regalia.

invested for decades and decades until finally it emerges from the
pocket and is used for living expenses. You do start paying tax when it
finally reappears, but only in dribbles. You have postponed for decades
the tax you would otherwise have had to pay currently. And you've got
the bulletproof asset there for an emergency, although you do have to
pay a penalty in the event of premature withdrawal. On the other hand,
a growth stock is *intrinsically* tax-sheltered.

To take an extreme example, there are fine growth stocks with no
dividends whatever, such as Berkshire Hathaway and Crown Cork. A
new client recently startled me by announcing with pride that he had
for many years held Berkshire Hathaway in his retirement portfolio. I
had to tell him that to me that was a nonsensical procedure: If he had
held it in his own fully taxable pocket, there still would have been no
tax to pay year by year, and he could die with the stock or give it away,
or at the worst pay capital-gains tax when he sold it. Since, on the
contrary, he was keeping it in his retirement pocket, when he took it
out, all that capital gain would suddenly turn into ordinary income! It
was the Philosopher's Stone in reverse: fiscally speaking, he was turning gold into baser metal. While there are particular situations when
this principle may not apply, it seems generally valid.

If one has assets in an IRA or other retirement fund, and if one has
other sources of money, one should consider postponing drawing on
the retirement funds for several years *after* retirement (although the
process must start at age seventy and one-half). This is to allow the
tax-deferred buildup to continue. However, a couple should spend
such assets during their combined lifetimes, because there is a double
tax involved in leaving them to their heirs: First comes estate tax, and
then the distributions are subject to income tax. By contrast, the appreciation of other assets at the time of death is not now subject to
capital-gains tax, just estate tax.

Passing Assets Down the Generational Ladder

Sooner or later one starts worrying about moving assets to one's children and grandchildren, to make it easier for them to do the very thing
one has done oneself. Here, particularly, the first rule is, *Start early*.
Many people save their $600,000 gift/estate-tax exemption until late in
their lives, or perhaps leave it to be applied to their estates. That's a
mistake! If you can afford it, you should use the exemption early, by
passing on enough to give your children their own nest eggs. *That way,*

the magic of compounding starts working for them straightaway, instead of the potential profit having to go through the senior generation's estate-tax wringer. Since taxes eat up around half a typical estate, that's a prodigious advantage. By the same token, a prosperous couple can start as early as possible passing on $20,000 a year per recipient, *as far down the ladder as they can reach,* notably to children's spouses and grandchildren. If you start early enough, this procedure will greatly reduce a taxable estate.

Of course, if later on you run low on money, you may have to look to your children for a contribution. By the same token, though, if the reason you run low is that you go bust or are sued, those assets will have been shielded from creditors and claimants.

Let the Kids Own Part of the Business

If you own a business, you can do wonderful things by making your children early shareholders. Suppose you are a successful magazine executive and have a great idea for a new publication. The usual formula is that you buy stock at a low price, and then offer stock to outside investors at a higher price. So, if to start things off you are putting up seed capital of, let us say, $200,000, why not cut in the kids? If the enterprise fails, too bad. But if it's a success, they will have created some real capital tax-free.

Family Regalia

By "family regalia" I mean nonincome-producing heirlooms: pictures, furniture, and jewelry that can scarcely be sold. Suppose, for instance, you have a portrait of Uncle Morris on the wall that is worth quite a lot now, but may someday be worth a great deal more. (My parents did in fact have a Sargent portrait of Uncle Morris.) Do not just write the child's name on the back of the canvas with a legend saying. "Given on such-and-such a date." The right way to handle things is to *sell* the picture to the children, or indeed grandchildren, today, for a reasonable price. The wrong way is to let it be taxed in the future in your estate at its then value—perhaps twenty or a hundred times higher. The gift may be challenged, and even if not, it will be consolidated with your eventual estate-tax liability. Matters are thus reopened on death, giving the IRS a chance to argue. So execute a properly notarized bill of sale, *with an appraisal attached,* in exchange for IOUs from the children involved. These IOUs can then be given back without tax at a couple's permitted rate of $20,000 a year per recipient. Everything is tied up and sealed off.

The worst of all worlds is when a family owns, for instance, a number of ancestral portraits, and none of this is done: The pictures are then taxed over and over again in each successive generation at the full estate-tax rate on the rising value. The same is true of furniture, jewelry, or any other such nonincome-producing asset. You end up paying tax amounting to innumerable times the original value. It would indeed often be better, at the price of sentiment, if instead of putting such property through an infinite succession of estate-tax bites, the family just gave it away. I still possess the huge, complicated repeater watch that J. P. Morgan gave my grandfather when they became partners. It sits in a safe-deposit box. My children have never seen it. In strict financial logic I should sell it to them as I've described or donate it to the Morgan Library, rather than have the family pay taxes on it endlessly.

Planned Giving

Not infrequently I will talk to a childless couple who plan to leave their assets to a charity, such as their old school or college. Really, though, it often makes more sense to make the gift now, reserving a life interest in the asset. This is called a *charitable remainder trust*. That way they get a tax deduction today, when it can improve their standard of living, rather than in their estate, when it can't. There are, in fact, a thousand cat's-cradle games one can play with assets destined for a tax-exempt institution, including charitable *lead* trusts, and it's an excellent idea to consult the planned giving people. Along with some undesired mailings you'll receive good ideas, and much kindly attention from the institution's trustees. Few relationships are more satisfying than involvement today with a charitable cause that you are going to make a large gift to in the future.

Family Capital

In this country, family money is often transmitted through trusts, usually managed by banks or law firms. From time to time a trust officer writes metallic letters, often prepared by computer, to the beneficiaries, who may never actually meet him.

When families that should be drawn together by their common ownership of the fruits of the older generations' labors and by their shared duty to transmit this patrimony to their successors are displaced by inaccessible specialists, they lose contact with their ancestors' life work, their dreams and sacrifices. The family tradition is reduced to a monthly or quarterly check. Indeed, this estrangement from family property renders it abstract and impersonal in a way that makes it easier for the government to take it away in the end. You defend your house or farm more vigorously than your remainder interest in a trust you know little about.

I do not mean that the family should attempt direct management of their family trust portfolio, only that they should keep an eye on what's happening and tell the trustees about their changing needs. Younger members of a family should almost never manage the family assets: They should understand and comment. *It's usually disastrous to confide family money, after the father dies, to an ambitious son-in-law*. In a spirit of rivalry with the absent patriarch, he falls into the cardinal heresy in investing, as in mountain climbing, adventurism. Investing is a serious profession, for sober, seasoned, careful older people, not an exhilarating game.

On the other hand, older-generation sole trustees are tempted far more often than is realized by improprieties that the beneficiaries only discover years later, leaving a bitter taste. So the correct arrangement for financial planning is family supervision of an outside trustee, or of a family trustee plus an outside one.

The ideal relationship between generations in dealing with family property comes about when children work side by side with their parents on a family farm or in a family business. They see clearly what's going on and their role in it, which can scarcely happen in handling a trust portfolio. One step in that direction is to hold regular family financial meetings, at which the family's situation and property—its hazards and prospects—are discussed and understood by all concerned. The meetings can be held during weekends in the country at the grandparents' house. The senior generation and all children above a certain age should attend, together with such professionals as lawyers, investment advisors, and tax accountants. Trust provisions and investment and tax considerations can be reviewed. Useful ideas often emerge. Easy questions can be answered on the spot, and complicated ones later in writing. Trust beneficiaries with interests different from the other family members can get their views heard. *(Often, trusts should be split into segments to reflect different needs or different residences.)* There can be informal contacts between the advisors and any individual beneficiaries who are diffident about speaking out in public.

Hold the meetings on a regular schedule whether it is convenient or not and whether there seems a reason or not. Otherwise, the custom will very likely lapse.

All this should help defuse potential resentments. With such full and open discussions, one can most easily work out intergeneration tax planning, such as timely gifts or sales of property by the older generation to the younger one. That's vastly preferable to waiting for the property to appreciate hugely and be devoured by estate taxes!

The senior or "income" generation often fears bringing financial daylight into these matters. I think that's usually wrong, for two reasons: First, the corpus of the money *does not belong solely to the income generation. It also belongs to the remaindermen.* The income generation are only the tenants of the house. And just as a landlord has the right to inspect his house at reasonable times while a tenant is occupying it to make sure that all is well, so, too, trust remaindermen should be able at regular intervals to see what's going on.

A second reason the older generation fears financial daylight is probably just a rationalization for preferring to keep a monopoly of information. They imagine that the grandchildren will turn into wastrels when they learn how well off they will some day become. At least as often, in my experience, the reality is the opposite. The young person who knows roughly what his or her expectations are begins to think like a proprietor, to acquire what was once called consequence. The grandchild kept in the dark sometimes becomes suspicious—perhaps with good reason—and eccentric.

When such an arrangement is proposed, the trustees may worry about the additional trouble and expense. Too bad. The priests in the Middle Ages similarly opposed the translation of the Bible into the vernacular: It undercut their monopoly.

One way a testator can assure that the professionals do not become unresponsive is by providing that a committee of the adult beneficiaries, or a designated outsider, often called the "protector," can remove the trustees altogether and designate others. That gives a lot of force to the family representatives in their dealings with trust administrators who have become sluggish or difficult. I know many families for whom such an arrangement would have saved a lot of money and grief.

An excellent strategy, as I discuss in a later chapter, is for a person of means to set up a *revocable* trust while he is alive and put his property into it. The trust becomes *irrevocable* upon his death or incompetence. Regular meetings are held by the settlor, the trustees, and the professional advisors, with the children attending when they turn a specified age, perhaps in their late twenties. *The whole structure can thus take form under the eye of the settlor while there is still time to make changes.*

The Executor's Job

It is virtually impossible today, given the complexity of our taxes, for a lay person to act on his or her own as executor of a large, complicated estate. Important things will be forgotten or mishandled, particularly postmortem tax planning. *In my experience it usually works best to nominate two coexecutors: a trust company or lawyer, plus a close relative who is trusted by the other beneficiaries and knows their needs and concerns.*

The bank (or lawyer) has the professional training and experience for this complex task, keeping things orderly and correct, and protects the other beneficiaries from possible imprudence or worse on the part of the family coexecutor. It will do all the technical work, including preparing the documents for the family executor's signature. The relative, who should understand the family dynamics and the reasons for the testator's wishes, will not ordinarily do any detailed work, but will keep the bank on the *qui vive*.

Unless it's agreed otherwise, both coexecutors are entitled to a full commission: they don't split a single one. A lawyer or a trust company will view an executor's commission essentially as compensation for collecting ("marshaling"), preserving, investing, and distributing the estate assets. Usually the commission would not cover the work of probate or of estate accounting. However, a trust company also provides postmortem tax planning, for which the lawyer usually charges separately, as well as custody service. Thus, one may get slightly better value by designating a trust company as the institutional executor.

Another advantage of a trust company is that it's a corporation, and so should still be there when the testator dies. An individual lawyer may retire or die before the testator, and the firm may change character.

A family lawyer may well give more imaginative advice than a trust company on estate matters. But there has to be a lawyer anyway, to handle the probate work and, ordinarily, to prepare the tax return. So his advice should be available even if a trust company is the institutional executor.

It is, of course, less expensive to name a family member as sole executor (or two members as coexecutors, in which case each should accept a half commission). He can appoint a bank as custodian and have the estate lawyer do the postmortem tax planning. This is a reasonable solution if the estate is not too complicated, at least one of the family executors has a quasi-professional familiarity with the job, and the family is closely knit.

The executor is nominated by the testator in his will but appointed by a court through Letters Testamentary. His duty is to settle the estate under the terms of the will, and until that has been done, to preserve the estate's assets as a fiduciary. Depending on what the will says, the beneficiaries can hold him liable for imprudence, such as losses from holding on unreasonably long to commercial real estate or to businesses run by the decedent, or for inadequately protecting or insuring property, or for improper distributions.

Here is a checklist of some of his duties.

Immediate Jobs

1. Find and read the last will and any related instructions, letters, or notes. Determine who the beneficiaries and fiduciaries are, and confer with any coexecutors.

2. Collect necessary information, consult the family, and take appropriate action on such anatomical bequests as the Eye Bank, and on funeral arrangements, together with obituary notices.

3. Arrange for the security of the residence, and if appropriate, the safekeeping of valuables.

4. Schedule a conference with the decedent's family, the estate's attorney, and any coexecutors.

5. Determine the immediate income needs of the family members and provide for the decedent's employees, including salaries or severance pay.

6. Get about twenty-five copies of the death certificate. (The funeral home will ordinarily do this.)

7. Tell the Post Office to forward mail, and cancel telephone and other services.

8. Cancel credit cards and club memberships.

9. Locate safety-deposit boxes, bank accounts, money funds, and securities accounts.

10. Send copies of the death certificate to banks, brokers, and the like, with instructions to conduct no further transactions, except to invest income and maturing loans in Treasury bills or money funds, until the will is probated. Find out what further documentation each requires.

11. Review insurance. (Change coverage as may be appropriate.)

Probate

The estate's attorney prepares and submits a petition to the appropriate court on behalf of the executor, requesting that the court certify the validity of ("probate") the will and appoint the executor through Letters Testamentary.

Depending on the state, all beneficiaries under the will and anyone who would have had an interest in the decedent's property if he had not left a will must be given an opportunity to challenge the will or the executor's qualifications. The attorney prepares for each such person a consent form under which he waives his right to challenge the will or to receive formal notice of this right (*notice of probate*). The court serves notice on those who do not sign a consent.

If there is no challenge, the court issues a certification of the will's validity and Letters Testamentary appointing the executor. If there are complications, the court may issue temporary letters to the executor, or to someone else, so that the estate's assets may be protected. The executor must then do the following:

1. With the estate's attorney, analyze the will and prepare a summary, together with a timetable of the estate's settlement, for distribution to the beneficiaries.
2. Review and sign the probate papers prepared by the attorney. Consider seeking preliminary Letters Testamentary if a delay in obtaining permanent letters is likely, or if the estate needs cash immediately.
3. Arrange for tax waivers from the state of residence, under which the state waives its lien on specific assets to secure the estate-tax liability.
4. Provide for ancillary proceedings if the decedent owned property outside of his state of domicile.
5. Negotiate the attorney's compensation, after the size and complexity of the estate are roughly established. It may be a flat fee, such as the equivalent of an executor's commission, or otherwise; hourly charges are not unusual.

Administration

1. Make an inventory of all assets, including the contents of safe-deposit boxes and tax shelters. Review the decedent's financial reports, incoming mail, and old papers for clues to assets. Value them at the date of death and the alternate date.
2. Transfer assets into the estate's name. (This is not necessary for real estate or personal effects.) Give any agents copies of the Letters Testamentary, tax waivers, and any other documents they need. Arrange for appraisals of the estate's assets for federal and state tax purposes.
3. Collect and review financial data, including canceled checks and checkbooks, investment records, income- and gift-tax returns, insurance policies, employees' salary records, closely held business records, medical expenses and medical insurance—all for as many years as appropriate.
4. Pay funeral and last illness expenses. Scrutinize all claims against the decedent, calling for appropriate documentation from the creditors.
5. Collect all benefits, including life and medical insurance, Social Security, Veterans Administration, corporate and fraternal-

order benefits, retirement plan assets, and notes and claims receivable.

6. With an accountant, establish a bookkeeping system to facilitate the formal accounting upon closing the estate. A professional fiduciary probably has an appropriate software package available.

Postmortem Tax Planning

1. Calculate the state and federal taxes, taking note of gift-tax returns filed, trusts in which the decedent had an interest or a power of appointment, foreign property, generation-skipping transfers, inheritances from others, and qualified disclaimers.
2. Determine whether any legatee should disclaim any bequest. This must be done within a specified period after the decedent's death, *and can be extraordinarily important*.
3. Establish the most advantageous fiscal years for the estate and any testamentary trusts.
4. Plan income-tax and cash distributions. This includes election of whether a Q-Tip trust should qualify for the unlimited marital deduction, preparation of the decedent's final income-tax return, allocation of income or expenses that can go either way (to either the estate or the decedent), meeting the cash needs of the beneficiaries, and spreading the income among several taxpayers—estate, trusts, and beneficiaries—to reduce tax.
5. Review and update the tax plan annually. Consider seeking an extension of time for the payment of the estate tax or income tax to avoid premature liquidation of estate assets.
6. File estate- and income-tax returns, using the date of death or the alternate date (six months later) valuation.
7. Obtain tax-clearance letters for the estate-tax return from the IRS and the state tax department.

Management

1. Establish liquidity needs; raise cash for debts, expenses, taxes, and legacies.
2. Manage the estate's assets; often, engage professional management. Keep cash working.

3. Take as active a role as necessary in closely held companies, real estate, tax-shelter deals, and ventures. Initiate or defend litigation.

Distribution

1. Pay cash legacies and other specific bequests, and distribute personal effects as soon as possible after probate. Where appropriate, arrange for professional advice for any family members who are unfamiliar with investments.
2. Once the estate taxes are estimated, make partial payments to fund trusts created by the decedent's will, and to residuary legatees. Enough should be left in the estate for estimated income and estate taxes, assessments upon audit, expenses, and contingencies. Distributions may have adverse tax consequences and should tie in with the tax plan.
3. Determine the investment objective of the trust beneficiaries. Arrange for the trustees to take charge of the trusts.
4. Have a final accounting prepared (the lawyer usually does this), and submit it to the court for approval and discharge of the executor.
5. Distribute the remaining assets.

I trust that after contemplating all this, the reader can see why for an estate of any size a professional fiduciary is indispensable as executor! It follows, incidentally, that an individual should hesitate before accepting a position as sole executor.

A Financial Inventory

Squirrels, I understand, forget about half the time where they buried the nuts they have collected. Amusing, perhaps, but people quite often forget too. I used to get letters from a savings bank about a cook who had worked for my family when I was a schoolboy. She would be about a hundred years old by this time. She was German, and eventually went back home to retire. I've moved here and there since those days, so it was quite an achievement of the bank to get these letters to me at all. They would advise that our old cook had an unclaimed bank account, which had been slowly accumulating interest for years and years. Since I have no idea where in Germany she lived, I have a distinct feeling that her children will never see that money.

From time to time one sees in the papers long lists of unclaimed deposits. Do you ever wonder how they were forgotten and what happens to them? They are rarely claimed. Probably many of the owners died without leaving a letter to their executor, lawyer, or next of kin detailing their assets, describing where their papers were and giving the guidance needed to sort things out.

And it's not only German cooks who neglect this precaution. Sometimes millionaires do too. W. C. Fields is said to have opened pseudonymous bank accounts all across the land, many of which are doubtless still unclaimed. Once a banker in Canada showed me a bunch of keys to safe-deposit boxes opened by Americans using noms de plume, probably to escape taxes. Apparently they had then died or forgotten about their boxes. The bank couldn't trace the owners by those false monikers, and if the survivors ever did come to claim the assets, they would have to prove that the person who originally rented the box habitually used that name—a hard proposition to demonstrate. So the Americans had been so careful that their families won't recover the funds.

Many states have an abandoned property statute under which savings accounts revert—"escheat"—to the state if the owner has not used the account for six years. In New York, the statute also applies to dividends on stocks whose owners have not made claim to them. Some time ago a lawyer friend of mine, Lisk Wyckoff, had a case involving Gray & Wilmerding, a brokerage firm which subsequently merged into Post & Flagg, which merged into Harris, Upham, which merged into Smith, Barney, which merged into Primerica, which merged into Commercial Credit, from which Primerica was later extracted again. When Gray & Wilmerding dissolved, there were some General Motors shares whose owner couldn't be identified. Over the years, due to an exception in the then statute, the dividends were paid over to the dissolved firm rather than escheated to the state of New York. Finally, a third-generation descendant of the owner, sifting through the gurry in his attic, discovered the documentation and made claim for the back dividends against Gray and Wilmerding, which by then had been defunct for thirty years. The way the statute was written he couldn't recover the dividends, although by a wonder he did get the shares back.

Often personal loans by a deceased person are conveniently forgotten by his debtors. It's notorious that all bills—frequently inflated—are presented instantly to an estate, while debts owed to the defunct are often considered payable in the next world at the earliest.

So the moral is, *do a financial inventory, and bring it up to date every few years*. Here are some of the items to include:

1. The location and numbers of bank and money market accounts, with the names of the officers familiar with the situation.

2. The location and numbers of securities accounts, and the broker, custody officer, or advisor.

3. Safe-deposit boxes, with a listing of persons authorized to open each box and a schedule of who owns what.

4. *An explanation for any large amounts of cash or gold in the box.* (Tax authorities attending the opening of a deceased person's

box like to claim that the booty represents undeclared earnings and then let the estate try to prove otherwise.)

5. The location of canceled checks or credit-card receipts, in case they are needed to document tax returns or rebut a claim that bills haven't been paid.

6. Information on charge accounts and credit cards—which should be closed out by the executor, obviously.

7. A schedule of what is owed to others, including mortgages and taxes outstanding.

8. A schedule of monies one is owed, detailing the circumstances, with documentation. (Note that demand loans are often extinguished by the Statute of Limitations if nothing is done about them.)

9. A schedule of life insurance in force, including "credit life," which pays off such obligations as car payments and mortgages.

10. A schedule of all other insurance. (Incidentally, every few years you should have your insurance brokers assemble a complete schedule, with suggestions on how your coverage can be improved.)

11. A listing of insurance that comes as an incidental benefit, such as through a business, professional association, or club. There may be free automatic air travel coverage if you pay with a credit card.

12. Benefits due from Social Security, the Veterans Administration, pension rights, profit-sharing plans, back salaries, deferred compensation, frequent-flyer miles in a family plan, and other business and professional payouts.

13. A list of where important papers are kept: your will, birth, adoption, and marriage certificates, naturalization papers, military records, diplomas, automobile and real estate title papers, copies of powers of attorney, and the like. All except the will belong in a safe-deposit box, since they can be burned or stolen almost anywhere else.

14. Payments that one has been in the habit of making to former employees, churches, charities, and such organizations.

15. Last wishes, such as funeral details and gifts to organ banks.

This financial inventory should be redone from time to time and circulated to one's attorney and proposed executors.

How to Use a Safe-Deposit Box

In August 1993, a diamond and emerald Cartier necklace was auctioned by the William Doyle Galleries in New York for $1.2 million. "If you can steal something legally, we did it," the buyers later exulted, adding that they expected to resell the necklace to a dealer for a fat profit. That dealer, of course, will in turn sell it to a customer for another hefty markup. In other words, the full retail value could be $4 million: a nice piece of change. But the previous owner will receive none of the proceeds. Indeed, she may never be known. The necklace had sat in a Citibank safe-deposit box for decades, rental payments on the box had stopped, and eventually, as New York State law prescribes, the bank sold the contents. Most of the proceeds escheat to the state.

The auction lasted six hours, and included the contents of four hundred safe-deposit boxes from five banks. The original owners have said goodbye to their property. Nice for us New York taxpayers, but *tant pis* for them.

What should be done to avoid this sort of disaster? Two things: First, tell the bank whenever you move. Second, as I've suggested, keep an inventory, periodically updated, of all your property.

Here are some other safe-deposit box situations I've encountered:

Monsieur Gotalot, textile magnate of Lyons, dies. Within hours his lady friend, Mademoiselle Fifi, is on the plane to Geneva. She waltzes into the bank, identifies herself to the manager, is escorted down to the safe-deposit vault, produces the key to M. Gotalot's box, empties the valuables into an unusually large handbag, and zips off. A few days later the newly widowed Madame Gotalot, draped in crepe and supported by a son-in-law, appears at the bank and asks for the manager. "My late husband always told me that if anything happened, I should consult you, monsieur," she whispers, producing Gotalot's passport and the death certificate. *"Oui, Madame,"* intones that dignitary. "Does Madame have the key to the box?"

"Mais non," stammers Madame. She is taken over to the Palais de Justice, where a judge issues an order. She returns to the bank accompanied by a *huissier,* a sort of bailiff. The whole bank party descends into the vault, where under the eye of the manager—who knows what to expect—and the *huissier*—who can guess—a mechanic solemnly drills open the box.

Empty! Is there nothing else? Nothing at all? *"Non, Madame."*

A chorus of lamentations resonates in the vault. All Swiss, all Swiss banks, this particular bank, and its particular manager are guilty of fraud, larceny, embezzlement, and grave robbing! The manager blandly waits for the storm to subside, has an underling usher out the unhappy widow and her escort, and goes back to work. The bereaved pair retire to a hotel bar.

This odd tableau is played out, with variations, every working day in Geneva, and indeed Zurich, Bern, and Basel. Also, however, in Detroit, New Orleans, Miami, Minneapolis, and Spokane.

Here's another: (The late) Mr. Kaushus turns out to have left his will, burial instructions, cemetery deed, and life insurance in his safe-deposit box. It takes several weeks before his family can enter the box through a court order. In the meanwhile his widow has to scrounge up the money to bury him in a different spot from the one he intended. (In some states, though, the next of kin can take out the will forthwith.)

Even sadder is the case of Mr. Sly. He doesn't trust banks. So he puts a lot of money in a safe-deposit box using the alias of Mr. Ebenezer. He dies, and his widow can produce the key, but not two witnesses to testify that her husband regularly called himself "Ebenezer." She may never get the money.

The opening of the Grabb family box is attended (as is the rule in many states) by a state tax man. With a smile he counts out $455,000 in hundreds that he finds in several big bundles, assuring the heirs that they'll have a chance to explain where it all came from.

Mr. Jinks's heirs are startled, on opening his box, to see a set of Polaroid snaps of that gentleman disporting himself in the altogether with a lady of the friskier ilk. An inspiring example for the younger members of the family, but dismaying for Mrs. Jinks.

Then we have old Mr. de Crepit, whose only son was killed mountain climbing. When he dies, his former daughter-in-law, now remarried, finds his will in his desk. She thought she was his heir, but to her dismay, it leaves everything to Harvard. Does she instantly ring up President Rudenstein with these comfortable tidings? Alas, not: she pops the instrument into the incinerator. Imagine her chagrin when a while later the bank, doing its duty, extracts from Mr. de Crepit's safe-deposit box a second copy of the document, and forwards it to the state Register of Wills, which in due course transmits the good word to University Hall. Mr. de Crepit had played it safe.

In general, safe-deposit boxes are for things that should be examined at leisure under court protection when someone dies, and for things one doesn't want to lose. They are not necessarily the best repository for valuables in general.

What, then, *does* belong in a safe-deposit box? Adoption, marriage, birth, and death certificates; citizenship, graduation, and military papers; deeds, car title papers, contracts, and important canceled checks; stock and bond certificates; such valuables as jewelry, stamps, and rare coins; unpublished manuscripts; very valuable guns; insurance policies other than life; photographs and inventories of property—so they won't burn up along with the house itself; and cash and gold, with documentation on their source.

It's best not to put in a safe-deposit box the only copy of a will, cemetery deeds, life insurance papers if there may be a hurry to collect, or a large sum in cash, unexplained. One probably shouldn't keep one's passport in the box, since one may have to make a weekend trip abroad, and there's no way to gain access outside of banking hours. Also, if lost it can be replaced.

Safe-deposit boxes are rented under individual, joint, partnership, corporate, or fiduciary contracts. If one joint renter dies, the bank must be notified before access is attempted. A joint contract in a state where the box is sealed upon the death of either party is often less convenient than a contract in the name of the younger spouse, who then appoints the older one his or her agent. That way, the box needn't be sealed if the older spouse dies first. Always record what in a box belongs to whom.

State laws differ. Here are some questions to ask: Does a surviving joint renter have immediate access? If not, how long does it take? Can the will or life insurance policies be taken out? How does the executor enter the box? Is a tax inventory required after the death of the renter? Does a lawsuit against one co-renter tie up the box?

There is, incidentally, an alternative that should sometimes be considered: the private vault company. There may be vault space available in a town where the banks are full up. Usually private vaults are open on weekends and they offer more privacy than a bank box, although less protection.

Two Good Uses for Revocable Trusts

Everybody in my business has encountered tough human predicaments like the two I am about to describe. They are situations many of us could face one day.

Old Mr. Appleton, a peppery octogenarian, had prospered in his trade of distributing building materials. He knew his merchandise backward and forward, forged solid relationships with reliable suppliers, and was trusted by his retailer customers. At seventy he became less active. By the time he turned seventy-five, he dropped into his office once or twice a week to check on things but had essentially turned things over to younger employees. Then he noticed that his memory was failing. He had trouble keeping his investments straight, mislaid papers, and found that people were paying less attention to what he said. Did he panic? No, he was a stouthearted and realistic old gentleman. "Everyone gets his run, and I've had a good one," he said.

But what should he do about his personal affairs when he could no longer look after them? His banker suggested a power of attorney to his son. No, Appleton's daughter-in-law made him uneasy, and he didn't like being under anyone else's control.

His lawyer came up with another alternative: When he thought he was losing his grip, he could sign himself into a conservatorship, which was subject to court review, and which he could cast off without court approval. His conservators—typically, family members—would in essence take over his affairs.

The worst idea would be to do nothing. Should his mind fail, his family would have to seek a court-appointed committee, and he would have to be certified incompetent, a humiliating procedure.

Few of us realize how common this situation is in an age when life expectancy continues to increase and when the specter of a nursing home lies at the end of the road for so many of us.

Eventually, Mr. Appleton and his lawyer determined on a standby trust. One was set up, with just $1,000 in it, and with persons in whom Mr. Appleton had confidence as trustees.

If his physician certifies to the trustees that Mr. Appleton can no longer run his affairs, then his personal property goes into the trust under the exercise of a durable power of attorney held by the trustees, who take over and run things for his benefit. Until then, there is no continuing expense. With this arrangement in place, Mr. Appleton feels confident. So what if he's a bit forgetful? He's enjoying life.

Professor Greenby had a very different problem at the opposite end of the age spectrum. His twenty-year-old daughter Emily was bright but hopelessly improvident. Money slipped like sand through her fingers. She couldn't refuse a touch from a friend or acquaintance.

She bought dresses that after a month she never wore again. She "invested" in paintings that belonged in a motel. She traveled to Europe with a group and was amply provisioned with traveler's checks, but twice ran dry and had to cable for additional funds. Her grandmother had left a trust that distributed capital to Emily's generation as they turned twenty-one, and the Greenbys (who were both teachers and had little capital of their own) had gloomy forebodings over what $1 million in one lump sum would do to their daughter. A couple of smoothies started making an investment of their own in Emily, taking her to nightclubs and turning her head with tales of jetting from Gstaad to Acapulco.

What to do?

One day the professor confided over lunch at the Faculty Club to the provost of the university, an experienced man. A week later the provost introduced the professor to his old family lawyer. A few months before Emily attained her majority, she, Professor Greenby, and the lawyer had a couple of good talks. Emily agreed that she did not want to be burdened with business decisions. She didn't understand business or investments and didn't want to. She knew she was an easy mark.

So she readily agreed to put her inheritance, when it arrived, into a trust to be managed for her benefit.

The instrument that the lawyer prepared for Emily, along with a one-page summary, provided that her trustees (her father and a trusted family advisor) were to invest the capital for her benefit and could make distributions of capital. Emily received all income. She could revoke the trust, but only with the consent of the family advisor. Such a trust has no tax effect. She would pay the income and capital-gains taxes in her own bracket, exactly as though she owned the money outright. But she couldn't spend more capital unless the trustees agreed.

On the morning Emily came of age, her father arrived at the breakfast table with the document. Emily signed without hesitation.

Both of these problems, or variations on them, are likely to be faced by anyone prosperous enough to be reading this book. The human dimension must be handled with tact and consideration. The legal and financial solutions are simple enough and readily available. But note that a revocable trust does not provide tax advantages, whatever you read in advertisements, only administrative convenience. That, however, can be exceedingly valuable.

The Last Great Tax Shelter

The law still lets you save a lot of tax by transferring a personal residence directly to your heirs through a *qualified personal residence trust*, or QPRT, also called a *residential GRIT*, or *grantor retained income trust*. This is an irrevocable trust into which the grantor places a primary or secondary residence, retaining the use of it for a fixed number of years. You can create two trusts for two residences. There's no minimum term, but the longer it runs, the bigger the tax saving. The amount of land you can throw in is limited to "adjacent land not in excess of what is reasonably appropriate for residential purposes," so you can't use a QPRT for a ranch or other large tract.

For gift-tax purposes, the value of the residence is its value when transferred, sharply discounted because of the grantor's retained right to occupy it. A dollar fifteen years from now is worth much less than today. There is a further discount allowed because of the risk of having the assets revert back to the grantor's estate if he or she dies during that period.

All this can amount to a huge bonanza, since in practice *your home is likely to be worth a lot more, rather than less, in ten, twenty, or thirty years from now;* and the estate tax will then rise to half of that *much higher amount.* The table below gives some examples of the federal gift savings at the 55 percent top bracket for a property worth $1 million today, and staying at that value. If you assume a higher valuation in later years, the savings are correspondingly greater.

While you—the grantor—continue to live in the house, you go on

Grantor's Age	Trust Term	Fair Market Value	Tax on Outright Gift	Taxable Value Using QPRT	Tax Using QPRT	Tax Savings
50	20	$1,000,000	$550,000	$207,683	$114,226	$435,774
50	10	1,000,000	550,000	482,774	265,526	284,474
60	15	1,000,000	550,000	260,089	143,049	406,951
70	10	1,000,000	550,000	333,903	183,647	366,353
75	5	1,000,000	550,000	552,276	303,752	246,248
80	5	1,000,000	550,000	470,401	258,721	291,279
85	3	1,000,000	550,000	567,915	312,353	237,647

paying all the usual expenses. You continue to deduct property taxes on your income-tax returns. You can also rent the place, which can be particularly useful for a vacation house, as long as you use it for the greater of fourteen days or 10 percent of all the days it is rented. (That would come to thirty-three days if it is rented all year round.)

If you want to continue to live in the house after the trust term, you must rent it from the remaindermen—usually your children—at a fair market rate at that time. This arrangement cannot be made at the same time the QPRT is established without risking loss of the tax benefits. You can, however, give your spouse the use of the residence after the initial trust term, and go on living there without this counting as a reversion of ownership.

Having your children as your landlords may be unappealing. One solution is to make the remaindermen an irrevocable trust of which they are beneficiaries. The trustee (or trustees) can be a friend or advisor who understands your wishes, perhaps together with one or more of the children.

If the grantor does not survive the trust term, essentially he is back where he started, without any significant penalty. The assets are included in his estate, with a credit for the gift tax paid or the exemption used when the trust was funded. So you lose only the cost of establishing the trust, plus interest on any gift taxes paid; also any opportunity cost, such as the possibility of using the transfer tax exemption for outright gifts. These are minor disadvantages.

Another is that the property retains its tax basis, increased by any gift tax paid, in the trust, whereas in the grantor's estate it would obtain a step-up to market value when he dies. However, there's a chance the step-up in basis in an estate may be eliminated in future legislation.

To show the effect, the following table gives the transfer tax savings in each of the earlier examples reduced by federal capital gains tax on the top 28 percent rate, assuming in each case that the property cost $250,000 and is sold for $1 million, its value when transferred to the trust, resulting in a gain of $750,000.

Grantor's Age	50	50	60	70	75	80	85
Gift tax saved	$435,774	284,474	406,951	366,353	246,248	291,279	237,647
Capital-gains tax	$210,000	210,000	210,000	210,000	210,000	210,000	210,000
Net tax saved	$225,774	74,474	196,951	156,353	36,248	81,279	27,647

In addition to these amounts, a family saves up to 27 percent (the difference between the top federal transfer and capital-gains tax rates) of the appreciation in the property after it is transferred to the QPRT.

Under current law, the grantor can solve both the tax and children-as-landlord problems by buying the house from the trust at market value just before it terminates. (Financing the purchase could be a problem if the property is a large part of the grantor's assets, although he could probably pay with promissory notes.) If that is done, the purchase price will pass to his heirs without capital-gains tax, since for income-tax purposes the grantor and trust are the same taxpayer. However, in deciding whether to form a QPRT, one should not count on this benefit still being available when the time comes to use it.

If the property is sold during the trust term, the grantor can pay any capital-gains tax with other funds, preserving the full value of the trust. If he is fifty-five or over and meets the other conditions, he can apply his $125,000 lifetime capital-gains exclusion on the sale of a principal residence to reduce the tax.

The trustees have two years after a sale to reinvest the proceeds in another house. If they don't, the trust has to pay the grantor an annuity, retroactive from the date of sale to the end of the trust term. Its remaining length does not affect the size of the annuity, which is based on the initial value of the retained interest (in the examples, $1 million minus the value for gift-tax purposes), the trust term, and an interest rate corresponding to the market rate when the trust was created. Here are illustrations, using the earlier examples:

Age	Trust Term	Grantor's Retained Interest	Annuity
50	20	$792,317	$ 72,480
50	10	517,226	72,286
60	15	739,911	79,198
70	10	666,097	93,091
75	5	447,724	108,028
80	5	529,599	127,784
85	3	432,085	163,446

One merit of the QPRT, compared to other ways of moving assets to the next generation, is that it does not reduce your income or income-producing assets. And yet it should reduce your taxable estate quite significantly.

You should consider whether a QPRT is appropriate, and if you think it may be, talk promptly to a specialized *trust and estates lawyer* about forming one. (This area is so tricky that one needs a specialist, not a generalist.) Although Congress specifically permitted the QPRT in the 1990 tax law, the administration may well decide to attack it.

Be sure to pay for a full-scale valuation of the property from a qualified appraiser. It should be ten or twelve pages long, with a complete description of the property and the area. It should list recent comparable sales, and discuss the pros and cons. *Don't even dream of relying on a summary letter from a cozy broker.* Your million-dollar house may be worth $10 million in twenty years, so you will have done the IRS out of millions and millions of dollars. If the original appraisal can be attacked, you must expect the worst.

Appendixes

Great Growth Stocks

A few years ago nobody would have believed it. Some of the best companies in the world are once again selling for one-digit price/earnings ratios, almost as though people were going to stop eating, smoking, and reading newspapers all at once, tomorrow. (In addition, of course, a lot of smaller companies that have been lost sight of by the institutions are selling at giveaway prices.) The April 1978 rally did no more than make a tiny dent in this undervaluation.

Thanks to the "smokestack" craze, the indexing fad, and today's preoccupation with yield, the most interesting stocks—those with earnings growing fast enough to offset inflation—are selling at an irrationally low premium over the run-of-the-mill industrials, very many of which should, alas, be considered as wasting assets.

In contrast, consider the newspaper chains, the pharmaceuticals, the specialty electronics companies; Capital Cities, Philip Morris, Schlumberger, and their ilk. They are generating torrents of cash: they have no depreciation problems, and both their earnings and their dividends (in some cases generous) are growing much faster than inflation.

As long-term investments these companies are in a different league from the standard cyclicals with profit-margin problems, labor problems, Japanese problems, ecology problems, and low unit growth to boot.

But you wouldn't know it from the prices of these superior stocks! Harte-Hanks Communications is eleven times 1978 earnings, Philip Morris nine times, and Schlumberger nineteen times, as compared with a nominal B-plus for the Dow Jones industrial average, which, taking account of replacement cost depreciation, should really be much higher: perhaps ten times? twelve times? fifteen times? A lot of our conventional, capital-intensive companies aren't truly making a profit at all these days.

On the other hand, it's not too much trouble to put together a list of outstanding growth stocks, with leading positions in strong industries, good recession-resistant characteristics, low payout ratios, and comfortable yields that have a total after-tax return well ahead of bonds and which you may not have to sell for a great many years, thus deferring indefinitely the capital-gains-tax liability.

The touchstone of common stock investment is IBM: If a growth stock is less attractive than IBM you might as well own IBM itself. IBM will have a yield of almost 5 percent on 1978 earnings and is growing at well over 10 percent a year. So your after-tax, after-inflation spendable income is about 3½ percent to 4½ percent, and growing much faster than inflation.

Historically, an attractive level to buy first-class growth stocks has been when the P/E ratio has been lower than the growth rate and they provide a comfortable yield. In the table below are some cases in which that prevails.

As usual, the better values are the issues that aren't fully understood by the investing community. If you own a portfolio of such stocks—and they are plentiful today—you can live off the steadily growing stream of dividends and face the future with reasonable equanimity, which is more than you can say for bonds or most industrials.

GROWTH AND YIELD

Stocks like these, with price/earnings ratios below the growth rate, offer investors a chance to keep ahead of inflation.

Stock	5-year Earnings Growth Rate	Recent P/E Ratio*	Est. 1978 Yield
Beatrice Foods	12	9	4.4
Block, H&R	21	9	6.0
Harland, John M.	21	9	3.2
Harte-Hanks	23	11	2.5
IBM	16	13	4.5
PepsiCo	15	11	3.1
Philip Morris	20	9	3.2
Pioneer Hi-Bred	32	8	3.7
U.S. Tobacco	13	10	4.8

* 1978 estimated earnings

A jazzier example is the series called "America's Fastest Growing Industries," published by John Herold in Greenwich, Connecticut. Over the last fifteen years the pooled earnings of companies in this series have grown 700 percent, the stocks themselves about 400 percent. Earnings and stock prices of the DJI have grown about 250 percent and 10 percent, respectively, over this period, only a fraction as well as Herold's.

Clearly, the growth issues are the ones to own, and in general their prices have reflected that. They rarely sell for less than twice the multiple of the Dow; at the peak in 1968 their P/E was 40 and the Dow's 18. Today, however, the whole "Fastest Growing" series is available for eleven times earnings, scarcely more than the P/E for the general market if you adjust for replacement depreciation.

Another example of the current cheapness of growth stocks is the T. Rowe Price New Horizons Fund, which is invested in higher-growth stocks. Over the last fifteen years the average price/earnings ratio of its holdings has fluctuated from a high of 40 in 1961 and 1967 to a low of 10 in 1974. Today it's barely over 10. Similarly, the new Horizons P/E was twice that of the S&P's 500 in 1961, 1967–68, and 1972. Last year it got down to the all-time low: a lower P/E than the S&P's! And today the ratio is only fractionally more than the S&P's.

Even after the sharp April rally, stocks like these remain as underpriced today as they were flagrantly overpriced in 1968–72.

Forbes, May 15, 1978

The compound rate of return of these investments for the next 15½ years, through 1993, ran from just under 16 percent to just over 25 percent, or an average of 18.6 percent excluding the bellwether, IBM. With IBM it was 17.5 percent. See the calculation following.

Growth Stocks

Company	Bought 15 May 78 No. of Shares	Actual Price	Price*	$ value	11 Sep 84 Price*	11 Sep 84 Value	shares purch. 11 Sep 84 with HHN $ proceeds	17 Apr 86 Price*	17 Apr 86 Value	shares purch. 17 Apr 86 with BRY $ proceeds	Value at 31 Dec 93 Price	Value	No. of Shares	# years	Compound rate of return 15.58 years
Beatrice Foods (1)	4.167	24.000	24.000	$100.00	28.125	117.19	1.835	52.400	314.49				6.002	7.850	15.72
Block, H & R	39.024	20.500	2.563	$100.00	5.625	219.51	9.176	10.875	524.18	4.131	40.750	2132.50	52.331	15.580	21.71
Harland, John M.	47.059	25.500	2.125	$100.00	11.875	558.82	4.346	22.125	1137.34	2.031	21.625	1155.55	53.436	15.580	17.01
Harte Hanks (2)	10.323	38.750	9.688	$100.00	40.000	412.90							10.323	6.300	25.26
IBM	1.504	266.000	66.500	$100.00	122.000	183.46	0.423	154.625	297.93	0.291	56.500	125.28	2.217	15.580	1.46
Pepsico	28.125	32.000	3.556	$100.00	4.750	133.59	10.866	10.250	399.66	4.383	40.875	1772.91	43.374	15.580	20.27
Philip Morris	22.939	69.750	4.359	$100.00	9.500	217.92	5.433	17.000	482.32	2.643	55.625	1725.20	31.015	15.580	20.06
Pioneer Hi-Bred	31.788	18.875	3.146	$100.00	10.500	333.77	4.916	6.500	238.57	6.912	39.000	1701.01	43.616	15.580	19.95
U.S. Tobacco (now UST)	67.845	35.375	1.474	$100.00	4.750	322.26	10.866	4.625	364.04	9.714	27.750	2453.78	88.424	15.580	22.81
Total				$900.00		$2499.44			$3758.53			$11066.23			

* Adjusted for splits
(1) Bought in a leveraged buyout by KKR in April 1986
(2) Went private in September 1984

Splits:

Beatrice Foods (BRY)	no splits
Block, H & R (HRB)	2:1, 10/85; 2:1, 10/87; 2:1, 10/91
Harland, John M. (JH)	3:2, 3/80; 2:1, 6/81; 2:1, 3/85; 2:1, 3/87
Harte Hanks (HHN)	2:1, 8/78; 2:1, 7/83
IBM (IBM)	4:1, 5/79
Pepsico (PEP)	3:1, 3/86; 3:1, 8/90
Philip Morris (MO)	2:1, 5/78; 2:1, 4/86; 4:1, 10/89
Pioneer Hi-Bred (PHYB)	2:1, 3/82; 3:1, 7/92
U.S. Tobacco (UST)	3:1, 1/83; 2:1, 1/87; 2:1, 1/89; 2:1, 1/92

The Man Who Never Lost

Everybody who finally learns how to make money in the stock market learns in his own way.

I like this tale of his own personal enlightenment sent by Melvid Hogan, of Houston.

"Right after I was discharged from the Army at the close of World War II and went into the drilling-rig building business, I began buying and selling stocks on the side, at first as a hobby. At the end of each year I always had a net loss. I tried every approach I would read or hear about: technical, fundamental and combinations of all these . . . but somehow I always ended up with a loss.

"It may sound impossible that even a blind man would have lost money in the rally of 1958—but I did. In my in-and-out trading and smart switches I lost a lot of money.

"But one day in 1961 when, discouraged and frustrated, I was in the Merrill Lynch office in Houston, a senior account executive sitting at a front desk whom I knew observed the frown on my face that he had been seeing for so many years and motioned me over to his desk.

" 'Would you like to see a man,' he asked wearily, 'who has never lost money in the stock market?'

" 'Never had a loss?' I stammered.

" 'Never had a loss on balance,' the broker drawled, 'and I have handled his account for near 40 years.' Then he gestured to a hulking man dressed in overalls sitting among the crowd of tape watchers.

" 'If you want to meet him, you'd better hurry,' the broker advised. 'He only comes in here once every few years except when he's buying.

He always hangs around a few minutes to gawk at the tape. He's a rice farmer and hog raiser from down at Baytown.'

"I worked my way through the crowd to find a seat by the stranger in overalls. I introduced myself, talked about rice farming and duck hunting for a while (I am an avid duck hunter) and gradually worked the subject around to stocks.

"The stranger, to my surprise, was happy to talk about stocks. He pulled a sheet of paper from his pocket with his list of stocks scrawled in pencil on it that he had just finished selling and let me look at it.

"I couldn't believe my eyes! The man had made over 50% long-term capital-gain profits on the whole group. One stock in the group of 30 stocks had been shot off the board, but others had gone up 100%, 200% and even 500%.

"He explained his technique, which was the ultimate in simplicity. When during a bear market he would read in the papers that the market was down to new lows and the experts were predicting that it was sure to drop hundreds of points more on the Dow, the farmer would look through a Standard & Poor's Stock Guide and select around 30 stocks that had fallen in price below $10—solid, profit-making, unheard of little companies (pecan growers, home furnishings, etc.)— and paid dividends. He would come to Houston and buy a $50,000 'package' of them.

"And then, one, two, three or four years later, when the stock market was bubbling, and the prophets were talking about the Dow soaring to new highs, he would come to town and sell his whole package. It was as simple as that.

"During the subsequent years as I cultivated Mr. Womack (and hunted ducks on his rice fields) until his death last year, I learned much of his investing philosophy.

"He equated buying stocks with buying a truckload of pigs. The lower he could buy the pigs, when the pork market was depressed, the more profit he would make when the next seller's market would come along. He claimed that he would rather buy stocks under such conditions than pigs because pigs did not pay a dividend. You must feed pigs.

"He took a farming approach to the stock market in general. In rice farming there is a planting season and a harvesting season; in his stock purchases and sales he strictly observed the seasons.

"Mr. Womack never seemed to buy a stock at its bottom or sell it at its top. He seemed happy to buy or sell in the bottom or top range of its fluctuations. When he was buying he had no regard whatsoever for the old cliché, 'Never Send Good Money After Bad.' For example, when the bottom fell out of the market in 1970, he added another $50,000 to his previous bargain-price positions and made a virtual killing on the whole package.

"I suppose that a modern stock market technician could have found a lot of alphas, betas, contrary opinions and other theories in Mr. Womack's simple approach to buying and selling stocks. But none I know put the emphasis on 'buy price' that he did.

"I realize that many things determine if a stock is a wise buy. But I have learned that during a depressed stock market, if you can get a cost position in a stock's bottom price range it will forgive a multitude of misjudgments later.

"During a market rise, you can sell too soon and make a profit, sell at the top and make a very good profit, or sell on the way down and still make a profit. So, with so many profit probabilities in your favor, the best cost price possible is worth waiting for.

"Knowing this is always comforting during a depressed market, when a 'chartist' looks at you with alarm after you buy on his latest 'sell signal.'

"In sum, Mr. Womack didn't make anything complicated out of the stock market. He taught me that you can't be buying stocks every day, week or month of the year and make a profit, any more than you could plant rice every day, week or month and make a crop. He changed my investing lifestyle and I have made a profit ever since."

I remind the reader that although this feeling for the rhythm of markets is a useful one to acquire, it's not the only strategy or even the best strategy. Probably Mr. Womack would have done as well by just buying and holding growth stocks.

Forbes, October 2, 1978

Becoming an Investment Professional

I am frequently asked about the best background for the investment business. To start with, I am quite sure what it *isn't*: majoring in economics, and then entering Wall Street. That's like recommending that an aspiring author should go straight from college into writing, or that a future saint should study theology and then enter church administration, or that a budding Casanova should start with a doctorate in anatomy. In all these matters one needs first to know the world and have practical experience. You invest in specific human operations: manufacturing, retailing, banking, technology ... a different affair from building theories out of figures.

And economics, like weather prediction at the turn of the century, is still a proto-science. It may become a real one, but does not yet meet an important test of a science, namely that it can be used as a predictive tool. Basic questions still mystify the experts. Nobody predicted the huge boom of the Reagan years, when industry grew by an amount equal to West Germany's entire economy and the stock market tripled. Nobody seems to be able to predict the price of gold, or what a higher yen will do to our trade with Japan. Most of our basic economic statistics are misleading, including unemployment, poverty, homelessness, and the federal deficit. George Soros, today's greatest investor, was trained as an economist, but decided that classical economics can't explain the stock market. Warren Buffett, another great, not only avoids economic formulas but says he does not even use a calculator. He examines *companies*, beginning with the people and the impregnability of the firm's niche or "business franchise." When I asked Peter

Lynch, who ranks with either of them, how much time he spends on economics, he replied, after some reflection, "A little less than fifteen minutes a year." So economics is not a particularly useful background for Wall Street.

Investment success requires above all a knowledge of business, which must include the ability to read and interpret figures, the language of business; a feeling for how people function; and a wide and deep judgment of affairs in general. It is almost indispensable to have some personal experience in business operations, which is what investment is about: A share of stock makes you a small partner in some enterprise. Ideally, you should have worked near a company's decision-making level, but at least you should have spent time out in the operating world. A few years with a management consulting firm is an admirable background, since you are plunged into a variety of different activities. Above all, since most things don't work, you learn how matters go awry. (They probably wouldn't call in a consultant if there weren't problems.) So you see a lot quickly, as with battlefield medicine. (I provide a cheerful compendium of follies in my book *Famous Financial Fiascos*.) I would rather hire a candidate with four years' experience at McKinsey or Arthur D. Little than one with a Ph.D. in economics. *Much* rather. How about business school, then? Probably helpful in business, particularly after a few years' experience outside, but the consensus in my set is that it's not a particularly efficient step in a career on Wall Street.

As to gaining a broad judgment of affairs, I share with Benjamin Graham, who founded the profession of security analysis, an enthusiasm for the Greek and Roman classics as a source of general wisdom. A 1990 survey of British business recruitment officers found that studying the classics developed "intellectual rigor, communications skills, analytical skills, the ability to handle complex information and above all, a breadth of view which few other disciplines can provide." Working word by word through the original texts sharpens the mind. You can't fudge it, the way you now can in many liberal arts studies. You are forced to submit to the material, which is also intrinsically enlightening. Thucydides may or may not be a great historian by modern standards, but if you master those fascinating pages you will understand better than most people how the great world, including NATO, functions. And Book VIII of Plato's *Republic* provides *indispensable* insights into how oligarchy moves on to democracy and then, via breakdown, to tyranny: Things haven't changed that much.

It is extraordinary how much rubbish is put about on investing, just as on politics, religion, and medicine. People want desperately to believe that there are shortcuts and easy solutions. In all these areas a substantial cadre of pundits has a keen vested interest in alarming you, and persuading you to hire them to put things right. Ecological perils, political perils, moral perils, medical perils. . . . It would be hard to sell newspapers whose pages reflected the reality, which is that things really change very little, being neither as desperate nor as promising as they may appear from day to day. The best way to get a feeling for all this is immersion in history, including intellectual and social history.

The thoughts on life of notable men are indispensable: Franklin, Sun-tzu, Montaigne. . . . Napoleon, whose reflections on statecraft should be studied with care, observed that the worst formation for a politician is politics: He should begin with much broader studies, or he will be of little value. Much the same holds for investment strategy, which is really a form of futurology. You need to recognize the patterns behind the changes in the world, and be able to evaluate with a cool and critical eye the enthusiasms then sweeping the investing community. There will be ample time to learn the details of the investment craft later, after you have the broader grounding in place. It rarely works the other way around. (For that matter, Book IX of the *Republic* urges that you learn about business *after* studying liberal arts.)

So much for the preparation. What about where you go to work?

Children of my friends or clients come by to ask whether, for instance, they should seek a job at Goldman Sachs or Morgan Guaranty. I always tell them that they should first determine whether they belong in the financial world at all.

People think in different ways: Some are thing-manipulators, some are idea-manipulators, some are leaders—people-manipulators—and so on. If you come from Cleveland, a manufacturing center, you tend to become a thing-manipulator: You're almost born at home with machine tools and jigs and dies. In Washington, D.C., it comes naturally to be a people-manipulator—to work in government. In New York, on the contrary, a young person is likely to go into idea-manipulating. This again splits into two main subcategories: literate people—who are attracted to advertising, law, journalism, and so forth—and numerate people, who will be happy in banking and finance.

So it is anything but clear that a young New Yorker should necessarily follow the well-traveled path into the financial world or the law. He thinks that way because he grew up there, but his true talent may be elsewhere.

For an insight as to someone's bent, I look at extracurricular activities. If the young person was editor of a college literary magazine, he or she will probably not be numerate enough for success in accounting, although of course it's possible. If he/she was head of the student council, it tells you something. So to get an impartial idea of your aptitudes, try the Johnson O'Connor Research Foundation, which puts you through a series of tests. They may well only confirm what you and your family already suspect, but even that helps. It is valuable, for instance, to establish more or less for sure that you're in the top rank of Americans in verbal aptitude, but in the bottom third of arithmeticians—or vice versa.

You might as well capitalize on your strength. Only a very small part of the population can expect to be really successful on Wall Street, and it's better to get an idea of your prospects before you start, rather than learn the hard way, by getting fired eight years along in your career, during a market contraction. Even more important than what your educational background and early experience should be to enter the investment field is the perennial concern: Know Thyself.

An Investment Credo

1. The basic purpose of investment is to buy a stream of earnings and dividends that will rise substantially faster than inflation: that is, to preserve capital in real terms and provide an income to live on.

2. Within this broad objective, active investment management seeks to buy undervalued securities that should rise faster than the market, and can then be sold in whole or in part to buy new undervalued securities.

3. We have a number of specific techniques that we follow when making an investment. Some of them are:

    (a) Normally, we want to know more about a company whose stock we buy than almost anybody else outside of management.

    (b) The stock should be misunderstood by the market at the time we buy it, for reasons that we also understand.

    (c) The imputed rate of return, assuming that one could buy the whole company at the market capitalization implied by the price per share, should be much higher than either inflation or the nominal return on bonds.

    (d) We only buy the stocks of outstanding companies that we would be willing to hold for a long time in the absence of any market . . . the way one buys a house. We do not buy unseasoned, mediocre, or troubled companies that seem underpriced: that is a more profitable strategy if it works, but increases risk if things go wrong.

4. Here are some of the characteristics of an outstanding company:

   (a) By nature it can float on the surface of inflation. This usually means that it dominates some particular area of a growing market, and is able to pass on price increases to its customers.

   (b) Management is superb, and dedicated to the shareholders' interest, with a substantial ownership position.

   (c) It is not a natural target of government regulation, consumerism, or intense competition (e.g., Japanese).

   (d) It has a high profit margin, and makes a high return on capital: in cash, not just in taxable accounting profits. In practice this usually means that it has very low debt, and also that it is the low-cost producer in its industry.

   (e) Typically, an outstanding company that is big enough so that we can feel confident we understand it, and still small enough to have a lock on something with dynamic growth, will have sales in the middle to high hundreds of millions of dollars, and will not be significantly unionized.

   (f) Often such a company will be a "productivity play"; that is, it enables other companies to make more money, rather than competing in the consumer market.

5. We do not employ margin. In a severe market decline, good stocks can be cut in half in a few months. If one is employing meaningful margin, one risks a wipeout, even though everything recovers in due course. That is even truer of short sales.

6. We maintain reasonable liquid reserves at all times, increasing them when we believe the market to be dangerous. Our cardinal objective is to avoid a major impairment of our clients' assets.

7. We do not regard bonds as a desirable long-term investment, unless one reinvests most of the income. If one spends bond interest during a period of inflation, one is to some extent really consuming capital, since because of inflation the value of a bond in real terms often declines at a rate comparable to the after-tax interest received. And above all, during hyperinflation bonds can lose most of their value in real terms.

8. One is, on the contrary, increasing capital in real terms if, for
   example, one owns shares in businesses whose value is building
   at the rate of 15 percent a year before inflation (or, let us say,
   10 percent after inflation) and one spends 5 percent of one's
   capital a year, even though the actual dividend income is only 3
   percent.

Bad Deals and Pitfalls

Speculative gambles and boiler-room scams prey on the greed of the ignorant. The pattern is standard, whether the subject is rare coins, heating oil, Florida lots, ranchettes out west, Canadian mining plays, Dali prints, commemorative coins or stamps, "limited" editions of ceramics, or whatever. The facts are misrepresented, and although all are warranted to go up, almost all rapidly decrease in value. I used to touch on them in columns, and include a few samples so that the reader can catch the flavor.

Commodities Trading

One of the meaner businesses since the British forced the Chinese to buy opium is going on today, on our commodity exchanges.

For most retail speculators, commodities—including financial futures, futures on stock index options and the like—are a form of gambling. And too many small investors are being drawn into them by promises of big profits on modest investments. Ninety-five percent of all transactions are just one speculator betting against another on whether a contract will rise or fall in price. Only 5 percent of commodity transactions are between parties that actually want to acquire or dispose of the physical goods represented by a contract.

The brokers take a commission both on the inception of the deal and its conclusion. These commissions typically consume a quarter to a half of the speculator's entire equity capital each year.

The trading volumes involved are immense: On a big day, the dollar value of contracts traded in soybeans alone can equal the value of all stocks traded on the nation's stock exchanges. The brokers' profits at the expense of the investing public—what Las Vegas and Atlantic City call the "win"—run in the billions of dollars annually. Yes, commodities is a profitable business for Wall Street.

But the purpose of investment is to put savings to work by owning shares in businesses that offer a satisfactory return, with the probability that the invested money will grow. Buying a sound bond provides a predictable yield. In commodity speculation, on the contrary, the underinformed outsider is virtually certain to lose his money if he keeps at it. From the results, the purpose of the system would seem to be to fleece the customer, not to help him.

It is sometimes argued that the commodity exchanges improve liquidity for producer and consumer. But the companies that acquire physical commodities for their own use—Hershey obtaining cocoa from Ghana, for instance—don't need the commodity exchanges to do this. They can buy what they need from the actual producer, directly or through the giant international trading houses.

I once did an extensive study of that rare thing, a highly successful commodity operator, Stanley Kroll, who made a lot of money for his own account after he stopped being a broker for others. In his fourteen years as a broker, he had worked for roughly a thousand customers. *Not one of them made money*, he says. Mr. Kroll told me that when commodity brokers discuss a customer, it is almost always assumed that he will be wiped out within six months to a year. In fact, the difficulties of making money in this business are so great that only about 20 percent of the floor traders themselves, who have every advantage, survive more than five years. The odds are worse than those for cancer, even though the professional can position himself on the floor of the exchange to profit from a commission broker's orders, as well as having instant access to news about both the commodity itself and who is doing what on the exchange.

A quarter of all commodity funds close down within five years, and half within nine years. The performance index put out by *Managed Accounts Reports*, the industry newsletter, calculates results monthly, so a pool that goes from 100 to 200 and back to 100 has a two-month average gain of 25 percent, not zero. And bad funds may not report their results. But particularly, "survivorship bias" distorts the results: What about the many funds that are "tapped out"? Dead men tell no tales.

Only a handful of the big brokerage houses have been scrupulous enough to resist setting up commodities departments. Most brokerages push commodities hard, since the commissions it throws off are large and lucrative. Thus, if a customer goes to Merrill Lynch or E. F. Hutton and turns to the right, so to speak, he gets serious advice on how to make money grow and provide a reasonable yield on the stock and bond markets. If he turns left, into the commodities department, he might as well have gone into a waterfront clip joint. He's unlikely to emerge with his cash.

One of the largest of the commodity houses, ContiCommodity, a subsidiary of Continental Grain, for years ran huge ads in the newspaper that, in a subtle reverse pitch, printed descriptions of "mistakes" that commodity speculators were inclined to make (as though there were a way to avoid the mistakes and get out of the quicksand). The ads described types of speculators who should not enter this market (as though any should), and listed "rules" for doing well (as though this were even remotely likely). Here are some of the company's admonitions:

"Keep reminding yourself on every position you take, 'My first loss is my least loss.' "

"Do not overstay a good market—you are bound to overstay a bad one also."

"Most people would rather own something (go long) than owe something (go short); it's human nature. The markets aren't human. So you should learn that markets can (and should) be traded from the short side."

"Recognize that fear, greed, ignorance, generosity, stupidity, impatience, self-delusion, etc., can cost you a lot more money than the market(s) going against you, and that there is no fundamental method to recognize these factors."

"Don't blindly follow computer trading. A computer trading plan is only as good as the program. You know the old saying. 'Garbage in, garbage out.' "

Very nice. But perhaps by mistake someone in ContiCommodity believed the company's own ads. The company set up three commodity mutual funds, which were snapped up by an enthralled public. All three lost so much money that they had to be closed down. (Still later giant ContiCommodity *itself* went belly up, and was abandoned, with a huge dowry to cover its loses, to another firm.

No, it's a gambling business, which, like Las Vegas, exists to take the customer's money.* It's unprofessional and a stain on the investment firms that deal in it.

The New York Times, May 13, 1984

Diamonds Are a Con's Best Friend

The category of high-pressure telephone sales operation called a boiler room preys on gullible speculators. They always have something new: In the old days, Canadian mining stocks, Florida real estate, Scotch whisky, vintage wine, commodity and option "programs," penny stocks, diamonds, coins, heating oil, Dali and other "art" prints, and all sorts of other collectibles. Many operate from California and Arizona. Some are based in foreign countries, including Canada and Holland. It really doesn't matter what the boiler room is flogging. The rallying cry is always the same: "So-and-so can only go up." That, of course, means that the victims are all buying together into a strong market; later, disappointed, they will be unloading into a market weakened by their own selling. Here are a few samples, to sensitize the reader to the genre. And remember the next one will be different, although the underlying approach doesn't change.

Diamonds come back into vogue every few years. Hustlers sell stones by mail, over the telephone, and through road-show "investment seminars."

Here's a headline from a help-wanted section of the Sunday *New York Times*: "Telephone pros . . . experienced only . . . sell investment quality diamonds." Applicants are furnished hard-sell scripts like this one (which is authentic): "LETS FACE IT THERE ARE NOT many commodities you can invest in, use and enjoy and 10 years later get back far more than you paid for them. AM I RIGHT OR WRONG MR._____? (wait for answer and continue). NOW I AM GOING TO RECOMMEND WE START WITH THE $2,480 PACKAGE. BASED

---

* One could argue that commodity speculation is different from Las Vegas because something *happens* in commodities: Goods actually move. That is essentially false. Even in trading "physicals," 95 percent of the transactions are just A betting against B. But in financial derivatives, an immense trading area, there is no question of a physical event. The bets are on currency movements, interest rates, or whatever.

There are a tiny handful of large-scale commodity speculators, armed with large staffs and elaborate computer programs, who make money for years; even of this category, however, most lose their touch in due course.

ON A 25% A YEAR INCREASE IN VALUE, WHICH IS A CONSER-
VATIVE ESTIMATE, THESE STONES WILL BE WORTH AT LEAST
DOUBLE IN THE NEXT FIVE YEARS . . . NOW WHERE SHALL I
SEND THE CONFIRMATIONS?"

The victims ignore the first rule of investing in something they are
unfamiliar with: Know Your Seller. Here are some of the splendid
fellows I encountered while looking into this hustle:

Rayburne Martin ran Tel-Aviv Diamond Investment, Ltd., of Scottsdale, Arizona. As Rayburne Wilson Hamilton he had been jailed for
embezzlement and violation of securities laws in Little Rock, Arkansas, which listed him as a fugitive from justice for parole violation. He
was found hanging in his jail cell by the Scottsdale police, so his wife
took over the business.

Harold S. McClintock (once known as Harold Sager), along with
Don Jay Shure and one other, was convicted of fraud in Chicago.
After that he and twenty others were charged by the Securities &
Exchange Commission with selling unregistered stock in fourteen
shell companies. He set up De Beers Diamond Investment, Ltd. Any
resemblance between this "De Beers" and the real De Beers of South
Africa is purely intentional; in reality, though, there is no connection
whatever.

You get the idea! And investing in diamonds through telephone
solicitation presents lots of other problems beside the characters involved.

1. The boiler-room diamond peddlers often pay more that ordinary jewelers do for their stones. They do not, of course, get them
directly from the De Beers Central Selling Organization.

2. They often charge huge markups; the customers ordinarily pay
more than the retail price, although they think they're paying less.

3. The "appraisals" that accompany the shipments are often made
by parties related to the seller and generally do not refer to realizable
prices.

4. When it comes time to sell, the customer will probably get less
than the current wholesale price. Yet he may well have paid several
times that price. So even if wholesale prices double or triple—which is
unlikely—he won't get his money back.

5. Some of the "diamond investment seminars" staged in hotels in
prosperous communities are sprinkled with shills.

6. After a diamond market bubble, supported by a wave of hustler-inspired retail speculation, the pendulum swings back. The hordes of small investors who bought because the stones were supposed to advance rapidly forever will be reminded of the origin of the expression "drop like a stone."

7. Who are they going to sell to? The outfits they bought from come and go with extraordinary rapidity. Mighty few are going to linger to face the wrath of their former customers.

8. And above all, diamonds—unlike gold, shares of IBM, or Treasury bills—aren't fungible: one diamond is not like another. Their value is subjective. Every sale is thus an individual, negotiated matter. When the bubble finally bursts, you have tens of thousands of distressed customers trying to sell into a sagging market, pleading with bored specialists who don't know them and are not really interested in their sad stories.

9. Contrary to what they're told when they buy, gem owners who sell at auction get little over wholesale price—usually about half the insurance replacement value they're hoping for—minus a selling commission.

If you can't resist, at least deal with someone you know to be able and honest. For most people that means your local jeweler, with whom you and your friends presumably have a solid relationship. He will probably try to discourage you from speculating in gems. In general, jewelers disapprove of this activity. If you overcome his resistance, he may agree to work for a limited markup. He will also let you have the diamonds appraised by an outsider before you have to accept them (which the boiler rooms won't). These measures will limit your risk, a cardinal objective in any leap into the unknown.

Forbes, September 18, 1978

Scotch Whisky

Most of the money sunk into Scotch whisky by small American investors responding to mail solicitation has been lost, and many of the transactions have been fraudulent.

The racket usually involves one or more of the following elements:

1. The whisky is sold for several times the going rate for whisky of similar quality.

2. Far from being supervised in bonded warehouses, as brokers indicate, sometimes no whisky exists at all. The promoter simply issues false documents.

3. Even when whisky exists, it often is not of the specified quality. For instance, many buyers are told that they are getting malt whisky, and instead are given grain whisky or a blend. In Scotland you can mix grain whiskies with less than one-third of 1 percent of malt whisky and call the resulting blend "Glengargle," or any other name that suits you. Unfortunately, the market for such an ad hoc blend is uncertain, since companies prefer to do their own blending.

4. If the whisky does exist, title is often not legally transferred to the American owners.

5. American investors have bought young whisky in the belief that it is "green" and will gain from aging. Actually, only a small proportion of the grain whisky used in blends is older than six years. After that, you can usually expect evaporation without appreciation.

6. Although whisky brokers have claimed that prices rise 20 percent to 25 percent a year, the price of aged whisky over the last twenty years has declined steeply.

7. There are continuing charges connected with the ownership of whisky, notably storage and insurance. If you don't keep up the payments, the whisky can be sold out from under you.

8. When you come to sell, almost nobody is interested in your cask or two, particularly since thousands of others will now want to sell their small holdings. It's as though you wanted to sell one barrel of crude oil.

9. If the investor does find a broker to take the product off his hands, he may wait a year or more to get paid.

Forbes, May 29, 1978

Train's Laws

1. Price controls increase prices.

It's more production that brings prices down. Price controls, by reducing profitability, inhibit production. Then the official supply dries up and a black market arises, in which more and more of the transactions take place. Thus, the black-market price, which is of course higher than the official one, becomes the real price. To maintain supply, the black market is increasingly tolerated. Things stagger along, with production lower and costs higher than they should be. It is no coincidence that in those American cities that have rent control the number of homeless as a proportion of the total population is highest.

It may also be true that price supports lower prices. I know that good farmers dislike price supports, which enable marginal farmers to go on producing beyond the economic demand for their product. This creates an oversupply that holds prices down.

2. Government costs twice as much and takes twice as long as the private sector to do any given thing.

Anyone who has been in government knows all about this one. Once I interviewed an executive in the New York City Partnership, a plan under which companies lend executives to the city attack particular problems. He was working on a big health program: billions of dollars. I asked him what proportion of this expenditure actually resulted in delivered health care, as distinct from administration and waste. "Eighty percent," he replied. "Very good!" I commented. "Do you really think so?" he answered, surprised. "Oh, yes!" I reassured him. Then a horrid suspicion crossed my mind. "Wait a minute," I said, "was that eighty—eight-oh—percent, or eighteen—one-eight?" "Eighteen," he replied. "Ah," I said.

I was not too surprised to read in 1993 that a study by the Institute for Civil Justice found that the Environmental Protection Agency spent seven times as much on overhead as on cleanup.

There are two main reasons for all this: First, the bureaucrat isn't spending his own money; indeed, if he hires more people he gets promoted. Second, the government has flawed motives: Politics comes ahead of efficiency. The investment conclusion from this is that direct or disguised socialization kills investment opportunity.

3. Nothing exceeds like success.

The truth of this law depends on what Professor Joseph Schumpeter called the "swarming of the entrepreneurs." A really good idea that becomes a big success will attract first two competitors, then four, then eight, then sixteen, then thirty-two, then sixty-four. In due course there will be an adequate supply of whatever the good idea is about, and then an oversupply, at which point the market price of that thing or service will decline. If the idea has been a rip-snorter, then the overpricing will be extreme, and the momentum of the decline may lead into a full-scale collapse, even a panic. Indeed, the true idea is often more dangerous than the false one: it will go higher and thus eventually have a more catastrophic fall.

This is why closed-end funds always go to a discount: If you have a good idea for a fund—biochemistry, let us say—so many will be formed that sooner or later the supply will exceed the demand. So, while the first few funds may sell at a premium over net asset value, later in the process almost all will sell at discounts.

The stock market itself is a perfect example of this law. The grossest excesses of a bull market will be based on a true premise that carries much too far.

4. Most things don't work.

It is usually accepted in the venture-capital business that about one plausible idea in a hundred pays off really well. One of my colleagues worked for some years in an "inventive research institute" that during his period examined roughly a thousand propositions. Exactly one (to do with telephones) was a big winner. In the ancestry of every successful company—the big three car manufacturers, for instance, or the major Wall Street firms—there are dozens and dozens of failures that were picked up for almost nothing by the survivor.

You could almost say that the purpose of capital is to be sacrificed to let society advance. One doesn't realize this, looking around, because only the survivors are visible.

The Shortest Possible Course on Reading a Financial Statement

Just as the language of music is notes, and that of poetry words, business events are reported in dollars. The basic news about a company is given in its financial statement, which is given in a conveniently stylized form, like a sonnet.

A company's financial statement comes in four parts: the *balance sheet*, the *income statement*, the *cash flow statement*, and the *statement of shareholders' equity*.

The first of these, the balance sheet, is in essence a financial snapshot of the company at one moment in time, the end of its fiscal year. It is generally brought up to date each quarter thereafter.

The income or profit-and-loss statement shows how the business did during the period: that is, sales minus costs.

The cash flow statement shows where cash came from and what it was used for. The amounts don't quite match those on the income statement, which includes, for example, purchases or sales on credit, where cash has not yet changed hands.

The statement of shareholders' equity tells how much the company's book value rose or fell during the period, whether because it made or lost money or took in new capital by selling stock. If the company made money, this statement will show how much of the profit was put back into the business and how much was paid out to shareholders.

A company's financial statement usually includes an auditor's opinion. A "qualified" opinion often indicates trouble.

The balance sheet is called that because it is set up to balance, like an equation: There's an implied = sign between the two parts. On the left (or "asset") side you show all the assets in the company at that moment—what it *owns*—and on the right (or "liability") side you show the company's debt—what it *owes*—*plus* the money that has been put up by the owners and kept in the business: the "shareholders' equity." If you think about it, the money you have invested in a house—your equity—plus the mortgage—a debt—perforce corresponds to the physical structure—the asset.

Here is an example: Suppose the shareholders of a company put up $1 million, which goes to buy $1 million worth of gold. A simplified balance sheet would look like this:

Assets	Liabilities + Shareholders' Equity	
Gold: $1,000,000	Shareholders' Equity:	$1,000,000

Suppose that we now borrow $1 million from the bank and buy an additional million dollars' worth of gold. Our simplified balance sheet would then look like this:

Assets		Liabilities + Shareholders' Equity	
Gold: $2,000,000		Bank debt:	$1,000,000
		Shareholder's Equity:	1,000,000
	$2,000,000		$2,000,000

In other words, the two sides of the equation still balance.

Good. Now suppose that during our first year of business the price of gold doubles, and we happily sell half our hoard for the original cost of the entire amount. Our simplified income statement now looks like this:

Revenues*:	$2,000,000
Less: Cost of goods sold:	1,000,000
Profit before tax:	1,000,000
Less: Provision for taxes:	250,000
Net income:	$ 750,000

We can use this $750,000 of free cash to pay down the bank loan, pay ourselves a dividend, build up our shareholders' equity, or buy

---

* Sales are ordinarily shown on an *accrual* basis—that is, what you are committed to—rather than a *cash* basis—when you actually take in the money.

back our own stock. Let's look at the first case: After paying taxes, we pay down the bank loan.

Assets		Liabilities + Shareholders' Equity	
Cash:	$1,000,000	Bank Debt:	$ 250,000
Gold (at cost)*:	1,000,000	Shareholders' Equity:	
		Common Stock	1,000,000
		Retained Earnings	750,000
	$2,000,000		$2,000,000

"Retained earnings" on the balance sheet is where you put money the company has earned and put back into the business, not paid out in dividends.

An interesting question arises when we add to our inventory at various prices. For instance, suppose that in our gold trading activities we bought at different prices and sold at different prices. The two major systems of showing these transactions are called "First In—First Out," or FIFO, and "Last In—First Out," or LIFO. When the costs of raw materials are rising, FIFO makes the profits look higher, since sales are taken against the earlier, low-cost, purchases. LIFO makes the profit look lower.

Footnotes to the financial statements may include information that does not show up in any of the numerical tables, such as pending litigation, company restructuring or prospective mergers. So always read the footnotes.

Perhaps the biggest difference between the way a businessperson and a nonbusinessperson examine financial statements is that if you have actually been in business you tend to look at the net cash and equivalents, and at the cash flow section of the report. If a business is doing well, cash will be building up and can be put to work in useful ways: paying off debt, adding to plant, buying back the company's own shares in the market. If things are going badly, the company will be short of cash, bank and other debt will be rising, and management will be run ragged coping with creditors instead of improving its products. (A hot growth company may also want cash because it has so many opportunities, but that's a more agreeable problem.)

After you have worked with financial statements for a while you get

*At market: $2,000,000. Assets are shown at the lower of cost or market.

in the habit of calculating the return on equity, how fast the inventory turns over, the operating profit margin, and a hundred other things.

So much for the Shortest Possible Course. To continue on your own, send to Merrill Lynch for its excellent twenty-eight-page pamphlet called "How to Read a Financial Report." (It may be that sooner or later their "financial consultant" will call.) After that, try Benjamin Graham's admirable *Interpretation of Financial Statements.* The whole thing is a lot more fun than you might think. And consider this: Even if you've only got this far, you're already well ahead of the mass of investors!

Investment Terms:
A Wall Street Dictionary

Account Executive: See *Broker.*

Accumulate: Buy on a large scale over time. Accumulation of a stock is said to occur if a number of institutions are gradually adding to their holdings.

Advance-Decline Ratio: This ratio, of NYSE stocks going up to those going down, is a useful barometer of the underlying condition of the market. Toward the end of a long upward sweep, speculative interest is concentrated on the few stocks that are still struggling forward, while the rest of the market fades, masked by the activity of those few. As the bull market approaches its peak, the number of stocks participating in the rise diminishes. So a graph of the number of stocks that advance each day minus the number of stocks that decline will normally turn down months before the Dow.

Against the Box: A short (*q.v.*) sale of stock that an investor owns but does not intend to deliver. This transaction protects the value of the investor's long position without giving rise to capital-gains tax.

Agency: An agency of the U.S. government. Agency paper is an obligation of such an agency.

Air Pocket: Said when there is virtually no support for a stock, so that in the face of selling it falls sharply on little volume.

American Stock Exchange (AMEX): Successor to the old Curb Exchange, which was conducted on the street. Smaller and less widely held companies than those listed on the New York Stock Exchange are traded on the AMEX or on the NASDAQ.

Arbitrage: Buying something in one market and selling it in another to take advantage of a usually small price difference. See *Risk Arbitrage.*

Asking Price: A specialist on the floor of a stock exchange always indicates a "spread" for a stock, e.g., 25–25¼. If you want to sell, he offers to buy at his bid price; if you want to buy, he sells to you at his asking price.

Back Office: Equivalent to the kitchen of a restaurant: the part of a brokerage house in which the mechanical functions are carried out, and which the customer does not see.

Bear: Investors who thought a stock was going down have long been called bears. The expression derives from a centuries-old proverb advising you not to sell a bearskin before you caught the bear. So stock sold *short* was said to be a "bearskin."

Bear Trap: When a stock declines, attracting heavy selling, and then surges.

Beta: The volatility of a stock as compared to the general average. A beta of 1.0 would mean that a stock moves in lockstep with the general market. But beta can be computed in different ways, and changes anyway.

Bid: See *Asking Price.*

Big Board: The New York Stock Exchange.

Bigger-Fool Theory: A risky investment technique, although effective when practiced by a master speculator. It consists of applying to the investing public the type of calculation that a skillful politician applies to the voting public. Just as the truth is often unpalatable to the electorate and unsound policies are often popular for a while, so too the reaction of the public to a plausible story about a company is sometimes easier to foresee than how the business itself is going to make out. The Bigger-Fool Theory investor knows he is not buying a solid value, but expects less informed investors—bigger fools—to take it off his hands when the time comes.

Block: A large stock transaction, e.g., 5,000 or 10,000 shares or more.

Blue Chip: A large, stable, well-known, widely held, seasoned company with a strong financial position, usually paying a comfortable dividend.

Boiler Room: A high-pressure telephone sales operation peddling dubious speculations to suckers.

Bond: A corporate IOU, typically bearing interest at a fixed rate for a definite term of years, and often backed by specific collateral.

The Book: A specialist's order book for a stock, in which he records offers to buy below, and offers to sell above, the current market price. A look at "the book" can be helpful in evaluating a stock's market position.

Book Value: The book value of a company is based on its financial statement, not on the appraised value of its assets. One takes the balance sheet assets of a company and deducts all debt and other obligations. Since assets often increase in real value because of inflation, while for balance sheet purposes they are depreciated, the book value of a good company may well be lower than its real value. For a company with obsolete equipment, both may be meaningless. "Hard book" means that all doubtful assets have been written down. Some of the best companies are in service industries, and typically have relatively low book values. See *Replacement Book Value.*

Bottom: In a major market decline, the point at which enough buyers are available to absorb all selling is called a bottom, particularly if it has been tested, and has held, several times.

Breakout: Movement of a stock above the highest price previously recorded.

Breakup Value: What a company could be taken apart and sold for.

Broker: A stock exchange firm's employee who deals with a customer; also called a registered representative, account executive, or customer's man. Some brokers are now called "consultants," which is deceptive, since it implies a professional obligation. Alternatively, a floor broker. Also, the firm itself, also called a brokerage.

Bull: A market optimist.

Business Franchise: A key investment concept. A company that is very hard to compete with because it has a lock on its market by virtue of a superior product, brand recognition, outstanding marketing or an advantageous location is said to have a strong business franchise.

CD: See *Certificate of Deposit.*

Call (Option): The right to buy a stock for a specific period of time at a predetermined price, for which one pays a premium.

Cats and Dogs: Third-grade stocks, unseasoned issues. Sometimes they go up very fast and sometimes they go down very fast. Since their future prospects are unknowable, they are not suitable for conservative long-term investors.

CBOE: Chicago Board of Option Exchange.

Certificate of Deposit (CD): An unsecured evidence of indebtedness of a bank, which may be sold to others, usually with a face value of $100,000 and bearing interest below the prime rate.

Chartist: A variety of technician who bases his forecasting on the formations traced by stock prices.

Churn: To trade an account excessively to generate high commissions.

Clearing House: A brokerage house that deals for other brokerage houses.

Closed-End Fund: An investment company with a fixed-equity capitalization, which does not sell or redeem its own shares.

Commercial Paper: Short-term unsecured corporate indebtedness.

Commodity: Agricultural products and raw materials traded on a commodity exchange.

"Consultant": A deplorable euphemism for a broker that falsifies the position. Consultants, including doctors and lawyers, stand in a professional relationship, a position of trust, to their clients, whose interest they must put ahead of their own. A broker is a salesperson, who stands in a commercial relationship to his customer. He is paid according to how much he sells.

Contrarian: A practitioner of a valid stock market approach popularized by Humphrey Neill under the name of "contrary opinion theory." In almost any market situation, one is safest acting against the current opinion. The term is also used to describe low price-earnings ratio investing—with some justification, since the stocks most in vogue, and thought most valuable, do tend to have high price-earnings ratios. While buying very low p/e stocks is not a particularly good investment strategy, buying the lowest p/e stocks in the Dow Jones Industrials works quite well.

Convertible: A bond or preferred stock that offers the investor the right to convert his holding into common stock in exchange for a lower interest rate than he would otherwise receive.

Correction: A minor movement against the major trend of the stock market. See *Secondary Reaction.*

Covariance: The degree to which one asset class moves in the market with another. For instance, gasoline prices and motels have a negative covariance.

Cover: To close out a short position.

Curb: The American Stock Exchange, which for years was indeed out on the street. When the brokers moved indoors, the number of colds increased.

Customer's Man: See *Broker.*

Cyclicals: Some industries are perennially subject to the vagaries of the business cycle: mining, steel, construction, automobiles, chemicals, machine tools, and the like. It is impossible to get away from the cyclical effect in business; just as there is always alternation between good and bad weather, so the cyclical type of company has an irregular earnings pattern, and usually an irregular stock price pattern.

Derivatives: Synthetic securities, such as options, manufactured out of such basic securities as stocks and bonds.

Discount Broker: A stock exchange firm offering a stripped-down service at a cut-rate price. Sometimes preferable to a full-service broker, since it is better not to be bombarded with purchase and sale suggestions.

Discretionary Account: One that a broker, investment advisor, or bank can manage without consulting the customer, usually under a limited or trading power of attorney.

Distribution: When stocks are passing from a few large investors, typically institutional, into the hands of many smaller ones; usually amidst much public excitement and unreasonably high prices.

Diversification: Most investors find it wise to own interests in at least ten different companies, and quite often in twenty or more. The Benjamin Graham technique of investment calls for even greater diversification, often into several dozen stocks. The limit was reached in Peter Lynch's management of the Magellan Fund, which often held over 1,000.

Dividend: That part of the company's earnings that is distributed to the shareholders.

DJI: See *Dow Jones Industrial Average.*

Dow Jones Industrial Average (also called the Dow, the Industrials, and the DJI): An index of stock market prices based on thirty large, representative companies. There are also Dow Jones Utility and Transportation Averages.

Dow Theory: Briefly, the view that market currents tend to move in major and minor trends. A major trend in the DJI should be "confirmed" by the Transportation Average, on the reasoning that improved business must be reflected in higher shipments, and thus better railroad and airline profits.

Down Tick: A stock trade at a lower price than the last previous transaction.

Drawdown: An odd euphemism for losing money.

EBIT: Earnings before interest and tax.

Economic Value Added After Tax: Return on capital minus the effective cost of capital.

Efficient Market Hypothesis: The fallacious theory propounded by academics that whatever can be known about a stock is at all times reflected in its price, and that it therefore does little good to study the facts. In reply I have developed the Efficient Professor theory, which holds that all available information is known to the academics, who therefore agree about everything.

Equities: Equities is another name for shares. The capitalization of a company consists of "equity"—ownership—represented by common or preferred shares (stock), and debt, represented by bonds, notes, and the like. (In England, "corporation stock" means municipal bonds, incidentally.)

Equity: The net value of a portfolio or a company.

Eurodollars: Dollar claims negotiated in Europe without passing through the U.S. banking system.

Exercising Price: The price at which the owner of an option has the right to buy or sell the underlying stock. (Also known as the *striking price*.)

Face Value: The amount that a note or bond promises to pay its holder. Not the same as its market value, which is usually expressed as a percentage of face value.

Favorite Fifty: A list compiled regularly of the fifty largest holdings of institutional investors.

"Financial Consultant": See *"Consultant."*

Finest Rate: The interest rate paid by the soundest issuers of commercial paper.

Fixed Assets: Plants, buildings, heavy equipment and the like.

The Floor: The trading area of a stock exchange, where the representative of the buyer meets the representative of the seller to complete a transaction.

Floor Broker: A broker on the floor of the exchange, who trades with other brokers, as distinct from a broker who deals with a customer. A "two-dollar broker" acts on the floor for a number of different firms.

Flow of Funds: Investing where you see the big money going. Really, though, a rationalization of the Bigger-Fool Theory, *q.v.*

Franchise: See *Business Franchise.*

Freewheeling: When a stock is making new highs, after having successfully penetrated a resistance area, then one says it is "freewheeling." Everybody who owns it has it at a profit. It is believed that the stock can then rise more easily.

Frontrunning: Improper trading of a broker for his own account ahead of a customer's order.

Fund: An investment company.

Fundamentalist: One who believes that the best investment results are obtained by studying the facts about a company and its industry and the economy in general, as distinct from studying cycles in investment psychology, or divining the future of the market by stock patterns.

Gap: If a stock trades at 20 at the close on Tuesday and begins trading on Wednesday morning at 21, a 1-point gap has opened. Wall Street lore has it that gaps are usually closed.

Glamour Stock: A stock that is exciting wide public interest at the moment.

Go-Go: Said of funds or managers who trade hyperactively in a booming market.

Good Buying: Said when a stock is being accumulated by strong, informed buyers.

GRIT: A grantor retained income trust. The residential GRIT, or qualified personal residence trust (QPRT), is discussed in the text.

Gunslinger: A go-go money manager.

Head and Shoulders (top or bottom): The formation said to exist when a stock has rebounded three times from a resistance level.

Hedge: To counterbalance your risk.

Hedge Fund: An investing partnership intended to invest either on the long side or on the short side of the market, or both at once. The theory is that it will be on the long side when the market is going up and on the short side when it is going down. Another theory is that if the manager has no opinion on the overall market, he can be long the stocks he likes and short the stocks he dislikes, and so make money in both directions. Few managers can actually perform this stunt.

Hedging: Typically, going short a stock to balance a long position.

Hot Issue: A newly issued stock that is in strong demand; often it will go to a premium over its original issue price.

Indenture: The text of a bond.

Index: Any of a number of stock market averages, including the Dow Jones Industrial Average, the Standard and Poor's 500, the Wilshire 5000, or whatever. There are also indices for bonds, interest rates, the major foreign exchanges, commodities, and, more recently, for categories of art.

Indexing: A popular but feeble theory among institutional portfolio managers. It holds that since their portfolios rarely beat the averages, matters can be improved by investing to follow the performance of the averages themselves. What would in fact achieve this effect is owning a diversified portfolio and doing nothing; that, however, would obviate the functions of the portfolio managers in question. Instead, therefore, they devise computerized systems of building portfolios whose performance will closely follow whichever average they index to. Since the composition and weighting of the major averages change regularly, this creates movement, expense, and a function for the portfolio manager. It thus slightly impairs performance, and begs the question of whether certain types of stock, e.g., high income or low income, may not be more suitable for the portfolio in question.

In the Money: Said of an option when the underlying stock is selling for more than the exercising price.

Institution: A bank, investment company, investment advisor, insurance company, or other large pool of investment buying power.

Institutional Broker: A broker who deals with institutions.

Inverted Yield Curve: When short-term rates are higher than long-term rates.

Investment Company (also called a Mutual Fund): A company registered under the Investment Company Act of 1930, which provides that in the proper circumstances a company whose only activity is investing need not pay corporate tax. Such companies are very closely supervised by the Securities and Exchange Commission. If an investment company continuously offers its stock to the public and also redeems it from shareholders who wish to sell, it is said to be open-ended, and if it has a fixed capitalization it is said to be closed-ended.

IPO: An initial public offering; the first time a company sells its stock to the public. IPOs are very often overpriced, and when they are almost all going to a premium, the market itself is probably overpriced.

Kicker: See *Warrant.* Typically, an equity bonus to "sweeten" a bond deal.

LBO: See *Leveraged Buyout.*

Leveraged Buyout (LBO): When an investment group, often allied to management, buys all the stock in a public company, thus taking it private.

Letter Stock (or Investment Letter Stock): In the latter days of a bull market, some buyers, including hedge funds and even institutions, are willing to buy stock directly from a company without the benefit of a prospectus or a public issue. They get a discount from the quoted market—often from 20 to 40 percent. The SEC requires that the buyer give the seller a letter stating that unregistered stock is being bought for investment, and also requires that it be held for a considerable period of time, usually about two years, to indicate bona fides.

Leverage: Leverage (in England, "gearing") is of two sorts: *financial leverage* and *sales leverage.* Financial leverage exists if a company is capitalized half in stock and half in bonds, for instance. A 10 percent increase in profits will produce roughly a 20 percent increase in earnings per share, since there are only half as many shares as there would be if the company's capital was entirely in common stock; and by the same token, if earnings decline, then earnings per share will decline more.

Sales leverage occurs when a company is operating near the break-even point, so that a small increase in sales produces a proportionately larger increase in profits.

Line: (Obs.) The old-time operators spoke of being long a "line" of "Steel" or "Motors," or whatever.

Liquidity: The extent to which a stock trades widely in the market, and can thus be purchased or sold without overly influencing its price. Also, a company's net assets, particularly in cash or cash equivalents.

Listing: A stock or bond's admission to trading rights on the New York or another stock exchange, based on its record of size, profitability, degree of public ownership, etc.

Load: The commission applied to the sale of a mutual fund.

Long: To be long a stock simply means that you own it.

Long Term: Either that period of time which qualified a holding for this category of tax treatment, or else a considerable period of time.

Margin: The percentage of the purchase price that an investor must produce in cash to hold the stock at a brokerage house. From time to time permissible margin is raised to discourage speculation, or lowered to encourage public participation in the stock market.

Margin Call: When a stock or commodity declines to the point where it is about to fall below the required margin, it "touches of" a margin call, meaning that the broker demands additional collateral from the investor, failing which his stock or commodity position is sold in the market.

Mark to Market: To value a stock or bond at its current market price, as distinct from its cost or face value.

Market Analysis: Great tides flow in the market, and an unemotional investor may be able to improve his odds by taking them into account. In the euphoric times when almost every new issue goes to a premium, when the cats and dogs are twenty times earnings, when everybody you meet is bullish, the veteran sells out and goes to Europe. In the midst of utter gloom, when sound values are being jettisoned because they are "going lower," when many companies sell in the market for less than their cash in the bank, and the subscription services are bearish, he reappears with his usual bushel basket and sweeps in the bargains.

Of course, euphoria can progress to a manic condition and gloom degenerate into despair. Nevertheless, it is helpful to know what the patient's current status is, as measured by odd-lot short sales, mutual fund cash, brokers' credit balances, net advances, and the like. They can be studied in figures or shown in graphic form. Such graphs are like those produced by a lie detector (heartbeat, breathing, sweating, and so forth). They have nothing to do with the astrology of "double tops," "penants," and "rounding bottoms" that the so-called chartists play with.

Market Capitalization: What the market says equity of a company is worth: the number of shares outstanding times the price per share.

Market Order: An order to buy or sell without limitation as to price.

Modern Portfolio Theory (MPT): A crude approach to managing large institutional portfolios, based on deciding which way the market should go, what degree of volatility and other characteristics are acceptable, and then, using computers, choosing stocks with those characteristics.

Money Manager: See *Portfolio Manager.*

Multiple: Short for price-earnings multiple.

Mutual Fund: See *Investment Company.*

Naked Option: Usually, a call that is sold when one does not own the underlying stock.

NASD: National Association of Securities Dealers. (See *Over the Counter.*)

NASDAQ: Stocks dealt electronically between dealers.

New Issue: An issue of securities sold by the company itself, rather than by investors.

Nifty Fifty: See *Favorite Fifty.*

No-Load: A fund sold without a commission.

Noah's Ark Fallacy: My invention—not found in the text. Short for Noah's Ark Shipbuilding and Dry Dock Company. The hack analyst claims that the NAS & DD has to be a bargain at three times antediluvian year's earnings, even though the good days were intrinsically a one-time situation.

Odd Lot: A transaction of less than a hundred shares (except for a very few high-priced stocks, for which the number is lower). A trade of less than a round lot pays a higher commission.

Offshore Trust: A personal trust may be either domestic or foreign (offshore). If foreign, its situs would normally be in a country that does not have significant taxes on such trusts.

Oligopoly: A monopoly exists if there is only one supplier for a given commodity or service. In an oligopoly, there are only a very few suppliers.

Open End: See *Investment Company.*

Opening: The price at which a stock first trades on a given day (also called the *opening price*).

Option: The right to buy or sell a stock or commodity at a specific price for a specific period of time, for which one pays a premium.

Out of the Money: Used when an option on a stock or commodity has not become profitable.

Over the Counter: A market of stocks in smaller companies that are traded electronically between members of the National Association of Securities Dealers.

Par: Of a bond, the face value, typically expressed as a percentage, e.g., 98 or 102. Of a stock, 100 (rare).

P/E: See *Price-Earnings Multiple.*

Ponzi Scheme: A fraud in which a fantastic return in investment is promised, and for a while delivered by using later subscribers' investments to pay the promised returns to the earlier investors. The original Mr. Ponzi said he had discovered a wrinkle in the use of international postal reply coupons that enabled him to deliver a very high return on funds confided to him. At the height of the excitement he had bags and bags full of money piled up on the floors of his collecting offices. In due course, of course, it all collapsed.

The market itself during the blowoff phase of a bull market becomes a Ponzi scheme. People forget that all those jigs and dies and milling machines and brick buildings cannot be revalued by 30 percent a year forever.

Pool: A group of investors who, particularly before the existence of the Securities and Exchange Commission, banded together to buy a stock (or sell it short) to attract public interest, and then sell out to (or buy back from) the public during that interest.

Portfolio: The generic term used of securities, like a *library* of books.

Portfolio Manager: The individual in an investment advisory institution who supervises an investor's portfolio, as distinct from a broker, who sells specific securities.

Position: A holding.

Preferred Stock: A class of stock with priority rights—both as to dividends and in liquidation—over the common stock of the same company. To avoid double taxation, corporations pay a much lower tax on dividends from their investments in other corporations (where it has already been taxed) than on business earnings. Preferred stock is usually priced at the level that makes it attractive to a corporation, taking account of this tax exemption. As a result, preferred stock is rarely a tax-efficient holding for tax-paying individuals.

Premium: The payment for an option.

Price-Earnings Multiple (also P/E): The number of times its own earnings that a stock is selling for in the market; e.g., if a company earns $3 a share and the stock sells for 30, the multiple is 10. In England, one would say that the stock's "earnings yield" is 10 percent.

Prime: "The prime" means the prime rate: the interest charged by banks to top-rated credits. (Some customers get an even more favorable rate, however.) Prime commercial paper is issued by this class of borrower.

Put (Option): An option to sell a stock at a given price for a specified time, for which one pays a premium; the opposite of a *call.*

QPRT: See *GRIT.*

Rate of Return: The internal or discount rate of return of an investment is that interest rate which applied to future earnings reduces them to the present market price.

Reaction: A price movement against the prevailing trend.

Registered Representative: See *Broker.*

Relative Strength: How a given stock is acting compared to an index.

Replacement Book Value: The accounting book value adjusted to reflect actual (usually postinflation) fixed asset prices.

Resistance Area: There may be something to this idea. If the chart shows that over a period of time a great many shares of a stock changed hands in a particular price range, and if the stock is now selling for much less, then it may be hard for the stock to repenetrate that range. You quite often hear someone say, "I bought Profits Galore, Inc., at 30 two years ago, and here it is at 10. I'm going to hold on until it gets back to 30, and then I'll kick it out." I suspect that the investor wants to punish the stock for its temerity after first getting it to confess, like an inquisitor.

Anyway, it seems plausible that vast numbers of disgusted stockholders waiting to sell may constitute an impediment to a stock's advance. (If so, this is an exception to my suspicion of charting.) When a stock they want to buy is approaching a resistance area, some people therefore wait until it gets decisively through before acting.

Retail Broker: A broker who deals with the public.

Retail Investor: I sometimes use this expression to describe a substantial but nonprofessional investor.

Reverse Split: See *Split.*

Risk Arbitrage: Ahead of a merger or acquisition, buying the stock of one company and selling the stock of another to take advantage of the difference between the market prices and the expected terms.

Round Lot: Generally, one hundred shares. See *Odd Lot.*

S&P: See *Standard and Poor's.* The S&P 500 is an average of the stocks of large corporations.

SEC: The Securities and Exchange Commission, which regulates all transactions in securities.

Secondary (Issue): A major stock or bond offering by an existing owner, rather than by the original issuer.

Secondary Reaction: A movement against the main trend of the market.

Short: When an investor, believing that a given stock will decline, sells it without owning it, intending to buy it, or "cover," later. To conduct the sale he must find a broker who will lend it to him until he covers.

Short Interest: The total of all open short sales, which is tabulated and published for each stock. A very high short interest constitutes support for a stock, since eventually all the shorts will have to be bought back, or "covered."

Short Sale: If one does not own a stock but sells it anyway, expecting to buy it back for less, one is said to sell short.

Short Squeeze: If the short interest is so high that the amount of trading in a stock does not permit the shorts to cover their position, then their own buying will force the price up—perhaps very sharply—making it harder then ever for them to cover. The short sellers are then said to be squeezed.

Short Term: For tax purposes, less than the period that at the time qualifies a purchase for long-term treatment. Otherwise, up to a few months.

Sideways: A stock is said to be moving sideways if its price changes little from day to day. The Wall Street community does not find this expression peculiar.

Specialist: A floor broker who in return for the right to keep "the book" on a company's stock undertakes to maintain an orderly market at all times by buying or selling if no other investor is willing to do so.

Speculator: One who buys an asset because he expects it to rise, rather than because he finds that the foreseeable stream of earnings, dividends, or interest is attractively priced.

Split: When a stock reaches an inconveniently high price, the management of the company will often split it two for one, three for two, or whatever, to create a smaller price per share, lower the total cost of a round lot, and make a larger number of shares available for trading. Sometimes the dividend is raised at the same time. A split is considered to be good news, but in fact has no effect on the intrinsic value of the stock. In a *reverse split* (curious expression), a low-priced stock is consolidated to increase the price per share. On the Canadian exchanges, such stocks are thereafter called "Consolidated" Gold Bug (or whatever).

Split Funds: Invented in England, and then imported here, these are mutual funds that have two classes of stock: income shares and capital shares. All the income of both classes is assigned to the income shares, and all the capital gains (if any) are assigned to the capital shares. If split funds can be created without limitation, the capital shares must necessarily go to a discount from net asset value, since new funds can be formed until the supply exceeds the demand.

At breakup, the income shareholders get their original cost back, and what is left over goes to the capital shares. Unfortunately, the net asset value per share may decline over 50 percent and the capital shares thus be wiped out, as has in fact happened. Split-fund capital shares are ultimately a gussied-up margin account, and the income shares amount to a loan secured by a stock.

Spread: See *Asking Price.*

Squeeze: See *Short Squeeze.*

Standard and Poor's: The most used manual showing the financial structure of large corporations.

Stock: A share in the ownership of a company.

Stop-Loss Order: An order left with the specialist to sell a holding when it falls to a specific price.

Straddle: An option to buy and a separate one to sell a certain number of shares of a stock at a specified price.

Striking Price: See *Exercising Price.*

Strong Hands: Substantial buyers, who one presumes will hold for a considerable period. The opposite of weak hands.

Tape: At one time stock transactions were recorded on ticker-tape machines. Today, the quotations are usually transmitted on an electronic display board, but the old term persists. The "broad tape" is the news ticker.

Tax Sale: A sale, usually near year-end, to realize a gain or loss for tax purposes.

Technical Analysis of Stocks: The technical analyst tries to predict stock movement through the shapes on a stock's chart, without reference to value.

Technician: Practitioner of technical analysis.

Ticker: See *Tape.*

Total Return: See *Rate of Return.* Another version of this expression heard in Wall Street is unsound, namely, the dividend yield from a stock plus the rate at which that yield is growing. For instance, if a stock yields 5 percent, which yield is growing at 15 percent, then the "total return," according to this usage, would be 20 percent. On the other hand, so would a 0.1 percent yield growing at 19.9 percent, which is a much less attractive solution.

Transfer Agent: The bank that handles the paperwork involved in buying and selling the common stock of a company.

Turnaround: When an investment banking firm or a new management group takes control of a troubled company, improves operations, and gets it back on a profitable basis. Very few investment banking firms are prepared to take on this job, which is one of the most constructive but difficult in the business.

Two-Dollar Broker: See *Broker.*

Volatility: The degree to which a stock is buffeted up and down by buying or selling interest.

Warrant: Option to buy a stock issued by the underlying company, often given as a "kicker" when a bond (or sometimes even a stock) is marketed.

Weak Hands: Speculative retail buyers of stock. See *Strong Hands.*

Window Dressing: Toward the end of a reporting period, mutual funds and banks will sometimes round their holdings to even thousands, or sell positions that have gone down and thus constitute an eyesore.

Wire House: A stock exchange firm specializing in retail brokerage.

Yield Curve: Ordinarily, long bonds yield more than short bonds. You can plot the yields for different bond lengths on what is called the *yield curve.* When short bonds yield more than long bonds, the yield curve is said to be "inverted."

Index